SYDNEY

Milsons Pt.

Balls Head

Morts

Goat I.

Ft. Macquarie

Ft. Denison

Garden I.

Bradley

Greenwich

Taylor B.

Sirius Cove

Woolloomooloo

Potts Pt.

Rushcutters B.

Clark I.

Darling St.

Double B.

Johnstones B.

Glebe

Annandale

Darlinghurst

Double Bay

Paddington

Surry Hills

Victoria Barracks

Darlington

Redfern

Moore

Botany Rd.

Macdonaldtown Sta.

Erskineville Sta.

Newtown

Macdonald-town

St. Peters Sta.

Alexandria

Carrickville Sta.

St. Peters

Waterloo Dam

Waterloo

Botanic Gard.

Waverley

Centennial Park

Race Course

Randwick

Coogee

North

SYDNEY
COCKTAILS

AN ELEGANT COLLECTION OF OVER 100 RECIPES FROM THE LAND DOWN UNDER

ALANA HOUSE

CIDER MILL
PRESS

BOOK
PUBLISHERS

SYDNEY COCKTAILS

ISBN-13: 978-1-40034-065-1
ISBN-10: 1-40034-065-9

This book may be ordered by mail from the publisher. Please include $5.99 for postage and handling. Please support your local bookseller first!

Books published by Cider Mill Press Book Publishers are available at special discounts for bulk purchases in the United States by corporations, institutions, and other organizations. For more information, please contact the publisher.

Cider Mill Press Book Publishers
"Where good books are ready for press"
501 Nelson Place
Nashville, Tennessee 37214
cidermillpress.com

Typography: Josefin Sans, Avenir, Copperplate, Sackers, Warnock

Photography credits on page 291

Printed in India

24 25 26 27 28 REP 5 4 3 2 1

First Edition

CONTENTS

INTRODUCTION

Bar 83 at Sydney Tower

Centuries before Sydney became a global cocktail capital, it was a town that was literally built with booze.

When the First Fleet set sail from England in 1787 to establish Australia's European settlement at Sydney Cove, its ships were stocked with a four-year supply of rum. The spirit quickly became the town's official currency—it was even used to construct a major hospital in 1811. Governor Lachlan Macquarie wanted to build a hospital in Sydney, but he didn't have the cash to fund it. Instead, he offered a contract to the developers that provided them with a monopoly on the importation of rum in exchange for building the hospital. The hospital subsequently became colloquially known as the Rum Hospital.

Cocktails weren't on the menu during those pioneering days. Thirsty settlers bought their spirits from makeshift "grog shops" and the only "mixed drink" was rum diluted by water. Governor Captain John Hunter began issuing liquor licenses in 1796 in an attempt to control the burgeoning liquor trade.

Early Opulence

In 1841, an enterprising man named William Wells converted his home into a pub and called it The Lord Nelson. Located in an atmospheric sandstone building in The Rocks district near the Sydney Harbour Bridge, it is the city's oldest continuously licensed hotel and has also housed an on-site brewery for the past fifty years.

Sydney Cove circa 1876

Fifty years after The Lord Nelson opened its doors, hotelier George Adams made international headlines by building one of the most opulent bars the world had ever seen. The Tattersall's Hotel was located in the heart of Sydney's central business district (CBD) and featured stunning mosaics, carved walnut fixtures, hand-painted and stained-glass windows, and extensive marble, with newspapers comparing it to the Taj Mahal. When the hotel was demolished in 1969 to build the Hilton Sydney, every section of the bar was painstakingly numbered, X-rayed, dismantled, documented, crated, and stored until it was time for them to be brought back to life as the Marble Bar, which opened in the basement of the hotel in 1973 and was retained during its renovation in 2020. Today, patrons can order a cocktail in surroundings that look largely identical to when Adams sipped whisky there.

Marble Bar

The Sly-Grog Years
and Beyond

However, it was another century after Adams opened his majestic bar before the modern Sydney cocktail scene was born. Its evolution was slowed by strict licensing laws during the first half of the twentieth century. While the city escaped the total ban on alcohol that Prohibition imposed on the United States, the New South Wales (NSW) government introduced a six o' clock closing time at hotels and pubs during the First World War as an attempt to improve public morality and as an austerity measure.

The Carlton Hotel bar, 1930s

The ruling was quickly nicknamed "the six o' clock swill," as it sparked a last-minute rush among workers to buy as many drinks as possible before hotels closed. Pubs catered to the frenzy by building longer bars, employing more staff, and tiling the walls and floors for ease of post-closing cleaning. A sly-grog (speakeasy) scene also evolved, with secret late-night venues, nightclubs, and illegal casinos springing up across the city. A referendum in 1947 to end early closing was rejected by voters, but the Supreme Court of New South Wales ruled that private clubs were exempt from alcohol restrictions, allowing them to trade alcohol legally after 6 p.m. A second referendum was held in 1954 and narrowly passed, with closing hours finally extended across the city.

Sydney Harbour, 1954

During the sly-grog years, an inner-city suburb called Kings Cross became the heartland of Sydney's illicit cocktail scene. The most infamous establishment was The Roosevelt Club, which opened during the Second World War and became popular with American servicemen and their Australian girlfriends. Gangster Abe Saffron took over

The Roosevelt Club in 1947 and flew in big names such as Frank Sinatra and Sammy Davis Jr. to perform. While the club's infamy eventually led to it being closed down, The Roosevelt reopened its doors in 2012 and now offers classic cocktails with modern twists.

The city also welcomed its first celebrity bartender in the 1950s. Born in New York City, Eddy Tirado moved to Sydney with his Australian wife and wrote numerous cocktail books throughout his career. He was a founding member of the Australian Bartenders' Guild and helped transform Sydney's Chevron Hotel into the hottest spot in town, when it played host to famous singers including Johnny O'Keefe, Shirley Bassey, and Nancy Sinatra.

However, there was a limit to how sophisticated the bar could become when there was only one brand of whiskey on the back shelf and the house "Champagne" was a local sparkling wine called Great Western.

The 2000 Sydney Olympics and the New Old Cocktail Scene

Sydney's bar scene burst extravagantly to life in the year 2000, when the city hosted the Olympics. More than 11,000 athletes, millions of spectators, and a host of international bartenders crowded into bars and clubs, which stayed open around the clock as locals and visitors partied. The music and cocktails flowed, and an era of innovation followed.

A bar called Eau-de-Vie Sydney revolutionized the city's cocktail scene in 2010. It brought the word "speakeasy" to an Australian audience and introduced them to wildly theatrical cocktail making. The bar moved from the city's east to an intimate, jazz-infused new location in the CBD in 2023.

The 2000 Summer Olympics cauldron in Sydney's Cathy Freeman Park

Now Sydney is a city crammed with secret bars hidden down corridors, in basements, and even behind faux cool room doors. It is also paradise for rooftop imbibers, with many pubs and hotels converting these previously disused spaces into stylish alfresco venues.

And then you will find bars on every level and street corner in between.

A Modern Movement Toward Sustainability and Terroir

Award-winning bartender Evan Stroeve says it feels like the city welcomes a new bar every week, each offering a different concept, idea, or purpose. Among them is his own first bar, The Waratah, which recently opened its doors in the inner-city suburb of Darlinghurst. According to Stroeve, Sydney bartenders are becoming increasingly focused on sustainability and provenance, with the city's cocktail lists championing local craft spirits and native ingredients.

"We're becoming more considerate of where we've come from, and where we want to go," he says. "The future is an exciting place to be drinking. More now than ever, Sydney bartenders are using their craft and cocktails to tell a story that extends beyond just spirit, syrup, and juice. Bartenders are working harder than ever to tell a story of 'place.'"

Sydney's bar scene features a combination of old- and new-world mixology.

The City of Villages

On the one hand, Sydney attracts global talent, who share trends from across the world and their perspectives on what works, what doesn't work, and what local bartenders can do better. On the other, a phenomenal pool of Australian talent finds its way to Sydney and collaborates with local distillers to find genuinely imaginative ways to use native ingredients in cocktails. Pearls of native finger lime take Mojitos to the next level, oyster shell–infused spirits add an ocean tang to Gimlets, and wattleseeds give a nutty flavor to Espresso Martinis.

Sydney, known as the "City of Villages," reflects its diversity in its bar scene.

"The industry is close and tight-knit," says Duke of Clarence venue manager Tom Joseph, "but it is built out of a dozen smaller communities of bars that have developed their own unique styles and cultures around each other. There is something for everyone, and everything for someone, somewhere in this city. And that's what makes Sydney great."

Those villages range from the precinct that surrounds the Duke of Clarence, which has been dubbed YCK Laneways (York, Clarence, and Kent Streets), to the historic The Rocks district, to beachside suburbs such as Manly, Cronulla, and Bondi, and to the bar scene in western Sydney, which is rapidly evolving as the city prepares to open its second international airport there in 2026.

Among the hundreds of world-class offerings to be found throughout the city, Maybe Sammy was named Sydney's best in the World's 50 Best Bars for 2023. The judges described it as setting the pace for bars in the country. The vision of its cofounders—Stefano Catino and Vince Lombardo—was for it to be a cocktail bar versed in the traditions and style of the grand old hotel bars of Europe and their pursuit of hospitality, updated with a little Rat Pack–imbued Las Vegas glamour and brought Down Under with some Italian-Australian irreverence. It is a philosophy that sums up the essence of Sydney's bar scene: a jigger of razzle dazzle and a dash of irreverence, mixed with some of the world's finest craft spirits and bartenders in the business.

How to Drink Like a Local

Enhance your Sydney sipping experience by sampling cocktails featuring finger lime, lemon myrtle, and lilly pilly (turn to page 288 for a glossary of Australian native ingredients).

It's also important to know the local drinking customs. For example, it is common to buy rounds of drinks for your friends, which are called "shouts."

If there's one word that describes Sydney's bar scene, it's eclectic. When the sun is shining, you might find yourself sipping a Paloma under the sails of the Sydney Opera House. When dusk falls, international hotel bars offer spectacular harbor vistas with a Martini in hand. As midnight approaches, an Old Fashioned at a small bar may beckon.

As you explore the city's diverse bars, some elements remain constant: the skills, creativity, charisma, and talent driving Sydney's unique cocktail culture.

How to Talk About Drinking Like an Australian

Australians have a broad and colorful array of slang terms for alcohol and drinking.

Having a big night out, for example, is often referred to as "getting on the piss" or "hitting the turps" (short for turpentine).

Wine is called "plonk" if it is poured from a bottle or "goon" or "chateau cardboard" if it's purchased in a box.

Champagne is "champers," while beer and spirits are called "grog."

Wine, beer, and spirits are purchased for consumption at home from a "bottle shop" or "bottle-o."

When toasting each other, Australians will, like Brits and Americans, say "cheers" or "cheers, mate." Aussies also have a longstanding tradition of using rhyming slang during toasting, so you may even hear Gen X-ers or Baby Boomers say "cheers, big ears," which will evoke one of two usual responses: "same goes, big nose" or "up your nose with a rubber hose."

Setting Up a Sydney Home Bar by Scott Allan

The Whisky List's Scott Allan has spent more than a decade working at Sydney bars, including NOLA Smokehouse & Bar, The Lobo, Assembly Bar, Trolley'd, and The Swinging Cat. At The Whisky List, Australia's largest online whiskey store, his focus is helping spirit lovers enhance their discovery journeys.

If you want to bring the flavors of Sydney's cocktail culture into your own home, it's important to know how to set up and stock your bar.

While you can repurpose cups or plastic containers as cocktail shakers and open corked bottles by inserting the base into a shoe and knocking it into a wall, there is no denying that having the right tools for the job makes the process easier and more satisfying. By arranging a small station at home that can be exclusively used for making drinks, you'll find yourself enjoying both the process and the result. In the world of bartending, much like the world of cooking, your workstation is your own zone and when it is in order, you set yourself up for success.

Two things you need to access quickly when mixing drinks are running water and ice. If you choose a spot close to these two things, almost everything else can be easily brought to your station. No bartender worth their saline solution leaves dirty equipment lying around, particularly when a quick rinse with hot water will render almost any piece of kit ready to go for the next cocktail.

Ice is the most fiddly part about making drinks at home. Often the number of cocktails you can make will be limited by the amount of ice you have ready to go. Professionals have the luxury of incredible ice-making machines that churn out perfectly clear cubes, together with deep stainless steel wells to store them, dedicated freezers for clear blocks, plus spheres and spears for those important final touches.

Fridges with ice dispensers are magic for solving the first part of this problem at home, otherwise you'll be stockpiling ice ahead of a party.

Ice for dilution doesn't have to be beautiful, but it has to be reasonably pure (filtered). If you want to go down the rabbit hole of clear ice, look up "directional freezing" and you'll find a ton of recommendations for how to achieve it at home, plus some products that do a pretty good job of it. Just promise me you won't make cocktails from bagged ice you buy at a gas or petrol station.

That's the basics covered, now let's get to the fun stuff. This is the equipment you need to get started:

✳

- Dedicated large chopping board with juice groove (no onion or garlic from dinner prep in your drinks please)
- 2 sets of Boston shakers
- 1 mixing glass
- 1 multilevel jigger
- 1 barspoon

- 1 paring knife (or other sharp, compact knife)
- 1 Hawthorne strainer
- 1 conical fine strainer
- Good quality waiter's friend (with a hinged corkscrew and a sharp knife)

And for those who want to get fancy:

- 1 julep strainer
- Cocktail picks
- Bitters dasher bottles
- Muddler
- Atomizer

- Squeezy bottles for syrups
- Tabletop ice bucket and ice scoop
- Sharp peeler

There are lots of great videos online showing how to use everything listed above, plus an endless list of recipes to try. Along the way, try my favorite whiskey cocktail, a Sazerac!

Your Spirits Starter Kit

When looking to stock your shelves with ingredients, I'd recommend starting with classic cocktails containing only a few ingredients—Martini, Manhattan, Old Fashioned, Negroni—and then branching out from there.

Ideally buy items that are likely to get a lot of use. If a recipe calls for a small amount of something obscure and you don't love that drink, you might just end up with a space in your cupboard dedicated to that one cocktail for a long time. Start with good quality spirits, but not top of the line. If you find you really like a particular cocktail, then try stepping up an ingredient and seeing if you like how the drink changes. Also be aware that some ingredients such as vermouths or other low-ABV wine-based products should really be stored in the refrigerator.

It's been interesting to see whiskey evolve as a cocktail ingredient in Sydney over the past decade. Not that long ago whiskey was seen as too complex and too strongly flavored to play nicely with others in cocktails, and many thought trying to do so was ruining the sacred character of the spirit. Thanks to innovative Sydney bartenders, we now balance, infuse, adjust, and create mind-blowing flavor bombs with every kind of spirit.

I recommend stocking whiskey with a slightly higher ABV than usual for cocktails. Most easily accessible products are around 40% ABV, and at this proof, once you add other ingredients, sugar, and dilution, their flavor is significantly reduced. You can regularly find American whiskeys at 45%, and Scotch or Australian whiskies at 46%, and I rarely prefer making drinks with products under this level. Cask-strength whiskeys can taste incredible in cocktails, but never underestimate their ability to cut your night short.

Top Tips for Ensuring Perfect Serves at Home

Find glassware that you love to use. It's a big part of the pleasure of consuming cocktails. You can revel in the way the glass feels in your fingertips and on your lips, the way it makes your drink look (in person or online), and even the sound it makes when you clink it with another in a cheers with a friend.

I also love having great mixers on hand when I don't feel like giving the cocktail tins a shake. I always keep tonic—which I love with Amaro—and soda for my Whiskey Highballs on hand in single-serve bottles, with at least one of each in the fridge. That ensures every serve is perfectly fresh and you're never throwing away a mixer that's gone flat.

Nick & Nora glass   **Coupe glass**

Low-sugar options that aren't artificially sweetened are great for letting the flavor of your chosen spirit shine and not putting you through glucose withdrawals the morning after. Don't be afraid to try some local options in this space, Australians have been doing drink mixers well for quite some time now.

The best skill you can develop when making cocktails at home is to taste as you go and balance your drinks before you serve them. Bartenders have their own thoughts on the ratios of ingredients in classic recipes, but all are trying to achieve a harmonious collection of flavors and sensations. If you taste your drink and it is too sweet, you can correct that before it goes into the glass by adding a touch of another ingredient or giving it a little extra dilution in the shaker or mixing glass. Once you can identify what a drink might need to make it a little more perfect, you can be confident in trying any recipe or even making up your own.

Old-fashioned/rocks glass   **Collins glass**   **Martini glass**

Opera Bar

CBD (CENTRAL
BUSINESS DISTRICT)

SYMPHONY OF
SAPPHIRE

APOLLONIA
NEGRONI

HOTEL NACIONAL

ALPINE GIMLET

SYDNEY SLING

CARROTINI

IN LIKE FLYNN

LYCHEE ENSEMBLE

HARBOUR BREEZE

THE QTT PUNCH

SUNSET SPRITZ

MENZIES BAR DIRTY
GIN MARTINI

MANGO MEZCAL
TOMMY'S

NEGATIVE GEARING

LOVE OVER MONEY

TROPICAL COFFEE
MARGARITA

23RD & BROADWAY

SUMMERTIME

SYDNEY G&T

BELLY DANCER

FIRESTONE

DRAGON FIRE

ELOPE IN A TUXEDO

KYOTO ROSE

GREAT ESCAPE

ARCHIE SAZERAC

FLYING FISH

RHUBARBIE

LOST IN PARADISE

THE GHOST OF PIÑA

GRAPES 'N' GRAPPA

MINI DRY MARTINI

SECRETS OF ALEJA

MORRIS
MANHATTAN

GOLD RUSH

MORRIS HIGHBALL

QUEEN MARGIE

Sydney's central business district (CBD) is encircled by one of the most beautiful harbors in the world. Its streets and laneways fan out from Circular Quay and are filled with hundreds of vibrant bars where you can order a world-class drink and soak up the city's laid-back vibe. The precinct is home to Australia's first town center, The Rocks, plus iconic landmarks such as Sydney Harbour Bridge and Sydney Opera House, the city's Chinatown, and the cosmopolitan Pitt Street Mall shopping district.

Nothing evokes "Sydney" more than the iconic Sydney Opera House. Located at the tip of a peninsula projecting into Sydney Harbour, UNESCO describes the building, a masterpiece of twentieth-century architecture, as a "great urban sculpture set in a remarkable waterscape." The Sydney Opera House has three interlocking vaulted "shells" containing two main performance halls that host an array of operas, concerts, and dance performances.

JAKE DOWN, APOLLONIA BAR

Apollonia Bar at Hinchcliff House is located just a few footsteps from Circular Quay in a moody basement space. Bartender Jake Down often finds inspiration for his creations in his surroundings—the concept for his Symphony of Sapphire, for example, was sparked by seeing the Sydney Opera House each day as he stepped off the train on his way to work.

"I remember observing my surroundings and thinking about the iconic nature of this unmistakably Australian landmark," Jake says. "When I was looking for inspiration for my entry in the Bombay Sapphire Stir Creativity Cocktail Competition, Sydney Opera House's visual influence fit perfectly with the brand's philosophy of 'Saw this, made this.'"

The resulting cocktail won both the competition and the hearts of cocktail lovers throughout the city.

SYMPHONY OF SAPPHIRE

APOLLONIA BAR
5-7 YOUNG ST, BASEMENT LEVEL, SYDNEY

Jake Down based his Symphony of Sapphire cocktail on the way the sounds of performances at Sydney Opera House can evoke memories, emotions, and feelings. He worked with the idea of synesthesia, the ability to associate sound with flavor and colors, to create the recipe, with blue symbolizing the note F# and green recalling A. The cocktail includes faux citrus and his own house-made "rain aroma," which captures the elements of Sydney's vibrant energy, nautical identity, and subtropical climate.

GLASSWARE: Ceramic vessel that echoes the colors of the
Sydney Opera House

- 1¾ oz. | 50 ml Bombay Sapphire London Dry Gin
- 1½ oz. | 45 ml young coconut water
- ⅔ oz. | 20 ml mint syrup
- 2 drops salt solution

1. In a mixing glass, stir all of the ingredients together.

2. Pour the cocktail over a piece of large block ice.

APOLLONIA NEGRONI

APOLLONIA BAR
5-7 YOUNG ST, BASEMENT LEVEL, SYDNEY

Tucked into the basement of Hinchcliff House, Apollonia is a cocktail bar with a focus on those seeking Negronis and romance. The dimly lit bar, an imagined Sicilian bandits' drinking den, is named after Michael Corleone's beautiful but short-lived Sicilian bride in *The Godfather*. The house vermouth blend gives the Apollonia Negroni its edge. It is cold-infused with dried Sydney banksia flowers and Bondi ocean salt (ocean water from Bondi Beach is cooked down until only salt remains and is diluted into a solution for the cocktail).

GLASSWARE: Old-fashioned glass

GARNISH: Paprika, nutmeg

- 1 oz. | 30 ml Widges London Dry Gin
- 1 oz. | 30 ml Campari
- 1 oz. | 30 ml vermouth

1. Pour the gin, Campari, and vermouth blend into a mixing glass.

2. Stir and then strain the drink onto a large block of ice in an old-fashioned glass.

3. Dust with paprika and nutmeg and serve.

HOTEL NACIONAL

DUSK CLUB
LEVEL I, EDINBURGH CASTLE HOTEL, 294 PITT ST

Popular late-night venue Dusk Club is located upstairs in the Edinburgh Castle Hotel. The bar was recently reimagined as a pop-up Cuban oasis with vintage-style artworks, rattan lampshades, moody lighting, blue velvet drapes, and lush tropical plants. Yuzu jam can be used in place of the puree if necessary.

GLASSWARE: Coupe glass
GARNISH: Pineapple wedge

- 1½ oz. | 45 ml Bacardí Gold
- 1 oz. | 30 ml fresh pineapple juice
- ½ oz. | 15 ml apricot brandy
- ½ oz. | 15 ml fresh lime juice
- ⅓ oz. | 10 ml yuzu puree

1. Combine all of the ingredients in a cocktail shaker with ice.

2. Shake, then double-strain the cocktail into a coupe.

ALEX RACLET, BAR 1880

10 BULLETIN PL, SYDNEY

Tucked away on Bulletin Place near Circular Quay, Bar 1880 is raising a glass to Australian publishing history.

The venue once housed *The Bulletin* magazine, which was first published on January 31, 1880, and produced its last issue in 2008. The publication featured influential Australian writers and artists who helped to shape the political and cultural landscape of its times.

The design of Bar 1880 was inspired by the magazine's history—restoring that timeless aesthetic while bringing in a mix of contemporary decor and old-world finishes that add warmth and character. Bar 1880

embodies a speakeasy vibe. Although no password or secret knock is required for entry, the bar provides an exclusive atmosphere with dim lighting, rich dark blue walls, and vintage touches.

The bar team is headed by former Zephyr manager Didier Nahum and 2011 French Bartender of the Year Alex Raclet. Alex cuts no corners with his drinks, as everything is made in-house from fresh produce selected daily to craft inventive signature cocktails such as the one that follows.

"There is a healthy selection of local and artisan spirits, with over twenty-five gins to choose from," says Alex, "which can all be made into a Martini for Martini lovers to work through over time."

ALPINE GIMLET

BAR 1880
10 BULLETIN PL, SYDNEY

Gin is huge in Australia," says bartender Alex Raclet, "and in the last few years, the dry Martini has become very popular in Sydney. A Martini is a fantastic aperitif to enjoy at any time of the day and if you love Martinis, you will love a Gimlet! It is sweeter and more vibrant. The Alpine Gimlet is our signature at Bar 1880, made only with Australian products."

GLASSWARE: Martini glass

GARNISH: Grapefruit zest, fern leaf

- 1½ oz. | 45 ml Australian dry gin
- ½ oz. | 15 ml Australian dry vermouth
- ½ oz. | 15 ml lime cordial
- 2 dashes grapefruit bitters

1. Chill a martini glass. Stir all of the ingredients together in a mixing glass with ice until combined.

2. Strain the cocktail into the chilled martini glass.

3. Garnish with grapefruit zest and a fern leaf.

SYDNEY SLING

OPERA BAR
SYDNEY OPERA HOUSE, MACQUARIE ST, SYDNEY

Sipping a cocktail at the Opera Bar beneath the sails of the Sydney Opera House as you gaze at Sydney Harbour Bridge is an unforgettable experience for any visitor to the city. According to the bar staff, if Opera Bar were a person, they'd like to think it would be Hugh Jackman—beautiful and just a little bit of a show-off, but in the best way. The Sydney Sling celebrates the city's incredible lifestyle, which offers opportunities to be outdoors by the water year around. The drink is made with all Australian ingredients, including Hickson Road Australian gin, which is produced just across the harbor from Opera Bar. The only secrets to ensuring the cocktail is served perfectly are lots of ice and the location—beside the water in the sunshine ideally.

GLASSWARE: Winchester glass
GARNISH: Grapefruit slice

- 1 oz. | 30 ml Hickson Rd. Australian Dry Gin
- ⅔ oz. | 20 ml Økar Tropic
- ⅔ oz. | 20 ml grapefruit juice
- ½ oz. | 15 ml fresh lime juice
- ⅓ oz. | 10 ml simple syrup
- 1¾ oz. | 50 ml lemon squash
- Orange bitters, to taste

1. Combine all of the ingredients, except for the lemon squash and orange bitters, in a cocktail shaker.

2. Fill the shaker with crushed ice and shake well.

3. To serve, fill a Winchester glass three-fourths of the way to the top with cubed ice then strain in the cocktail from the shaker.

4. Top the drink with a dash of lemon squash.

5. Further top the drink with crushed ice to create a crown.

6. Add several dashes of orange bitters to the crushed ice and serve.

ALBERTO SARA, THE BAR AT HICKSON HOUSE

The Bar at Hickson House is set in the historic Metcalfe Bond Stores in The Rocks and boasts its own distillery on-site. The distillery and bar are surrounded by the soaring brickwork and girders of the former garage of the multinational advertising agency Saatchi & Saatchi, which was once the infamous location for many warehouse parties.

CARROTINI

The latest release by Hickson House Distilling Co. is its Seven Spice Gin, a unique savory gin crafted specifically for pairing with food, especially grilled meats and seafood. Seven Spice Gin is a nod of respect to the diversity of Australian native botanicals. It features a delicate blend of seven local ingredients: native lemongrass, mountain pepper leaf, aniseed myrtle, finger lime, wattleseed, bush tomato, and lemon myrtle have been carefully balanced with traditional juniper to create a contemporary Australian gin. Alberto Sara and his fellow bartenders mix a flight of cocktails each night that have been created to highlight the savory nature of the gin. You can substitute any savory gin for a memorable Carrotini experience.

GLASSWARE: Martini glass
GARNISH: Small roasted carrot marinated in Lillet Blanc

- 1⅓ oz. | 40 ml Hickson Rd. Seven Spice Gin
- ⅔ oz. | 20 ml aquavit
- 2 dashes orange bitters

1. Wet-shake the ingredients with ice and strain the cocktail into a martini glass.

2. Garnish with a small roasted carrot marinated in Lillet Blanc.

ADAM LAU, GRAIN

Grain is located within the Four Seasons Hotel Sydney, steps from Sydney Harbour. While tourists stop into the bar for exceptional cocktail experiences, it has also developed a reputation among Sydneysiders for its personalized service. Bar manager Adam Lau says locals love returning to a venue where the bartender knows his or her name as well as their cocktail preference.

While Australians have been slower to embrace the hotel bar experience than other countries around the world, they are captivated by the sophisticated bar culture now on offer in the city's luxury hotels in recent years. Canadian-born with Hong Kong heritage, Adam grew up in Hong Kong before heading to Australia in pursuit of adventure. His bartending style highlights classic and vintage cocktails, with a distinct flavor or technique that puts a new twist on the old. He spends hours each week experimenting with new creations—his latest obsession is barrel-aged cocktails.

IN LIKE FLYNN

GRAIN
FOUR SEASONS HOTEL SYDNEY, 199 GEORGE ST, THE ROCKS

Adam Lau wanted to create a classic, approachable, and unique cocktail with an Australian influence and the result was In Like Flynn, inspired by the classic White Lady. The recipe took him almost six months to perfect and showcases native eucalyptus, which is an iconic smell and taste for Australians.

GLASSWARE: Coupette glass
GARNISH: Koala on edible paper (optional)

- 1½ oz. | 45 ml Widges London Dry Gin
- ⅔ oz. | 20 ml fresh lemon juice
- ½ oz. | 15 ml Amaro Montenegro
- ½ oz. | 15 ml simple syrup
- ⅓ oz. | 10 ml egg white
- Dash eucalyptus tincture
- Lemon peel, to express

1. Combine all of the ingredients, except for the lemon peel, in a cocktail shaker and dry-shake without ice.

2. Wet-shake the ingredients with ice.

3. Double-strain the cocktail into a coupette.

4. Twist a piece of lemon peel over the cocktail then discard the peel.

5. If using, set the circle of edible paper on top of the cocktail.

LYCHEE ENSEMBLE

MARBLE BAR
SYDNEY HILTON, 488 GEORGE ST, SYDNEY

Built in 1893, the Marble Bar is rich with history. Hilton Sydney Food and Beverage Operations Manager James Heggie says there are many stories to be celebrated and told within its walls. Sydneysiders love to celebrate at the Marble Bar and many guests have a connection with the venue—it could be where they met their partner or where their parents met; it may be that their singing career kicked off there, or it was where they saw their first music performance. The Lychee Ensemble is a favorite with patrons and has been on the menu for a decade. Heggie says using fresh lychee puree also ensures the perfect serve.

GLASSWARE: Martini glass
GARNISH: Dried rose petals

- 1 oz. | 30 ml lychee puree
- ⅚ oz. | 25 ml vodka
- ½ oz. | 15 ml fresh lemon juice
- ⅚ oz. | 25 ml lychee liqueur
- ⅓ oz. | 10 ml rose syrup
- 3 drops rose water

1. Add all of the ingredients to a cocktail shaker with ice.

2. To achieve a good mix, shake vigorously.

3. Strain the cocktail into a martini glass and garnish with dried rose petals.

HARBOUR BREEZE

BAR LULU
LEVEL 1, BAYS 4 AND 5, 7-27 CIRCULAR QUAY WEST,
THE ROCKS

Bar Lulu is located in the heart of the bustling The Rocks precinct, which is renowned for its historic buildings, weekend markets, and sleek bars. With its unobstructed views of the Sydney Opera House and Sydney Harbour Bridge, Bar Lulu exudes history and elegance. The Harbour Breeze cocktail is loaded with ingredients that signal "Sydney" and pays tribute to the coastal landscape by adorning the glass with a delicate sea salt rim (optional), which adds a touch of oceanic charm to the presentation. To celebrate Sydney's colorful culture, the cocktail is adorned with garnishes inspired by the city's thriving arts scene. It could be a vibrant edible flower or rosemary, a delicate herb sprig, or a slice of native fruit, adding a visual pop.

GLASSWARE: Coupe glass

GARNISH: Lemon peel, rosemary

- 2 oz. | 60 ml clear apple juice
- 1½ oz. | 45 ml Archie Rose Signature Dry Gin
- ⅓ oz. | 10 ml fresh lemon juice
- ⅓ oz. | 10 ml sugar
- ⅓ oz. | 10 ml limoncello
- ⅓ oz. | 10 ml Seadrift Wild Hibiscus
- ¼ oz. | 7.5 ml dry vermouth
- Barspoon blue curaçao syrup

1. Add all of the ingredients to a Boston shaker.

2. Place a Hawthorne strainer over one side.

3. Place ice in the other half.

4. Roll the cocktail four or five times.

5. Pour the cocktail into a champagne coupe glass and add your choice of garnish.

THE QTT PUNCH

CAFFE Q'S
R2OO2/5O BRIDGE ST, SYDNEY

S et between two monolith buildings at Circular Quay, Caffe Q's is an alfresco destination in the Quay Quarter development, which has rejuvenated this part of town and brought 10,000 extra workers to the precinct. If Brix Australian Spiced Rum isn't available, use your craft spiced rum of choice.

GLASSWARE: Highball glass
GARNISH: Mint sprig, orange half-moon

- 1 oz. | 30 ml Brix Australian Spiced Rum
- 1 oz. | 30 ml fresh lime juice
- ½ oz. | 15 ml Select Aperitivo
- ½ oz. | 15 ml grapefruit juice
- ½ oz.| 15 ml Crawley's Bartender Falernum Syrup
- 4 dashes rhubarb bitters
- Soda water, to top

1. Add all of the ingredients, except for the soda water, to a cocktail shaker with ice.

2. Shake and strain the cocktail into a highball glass.

3. Top up with soda and garnish with a mint sprig and orange half-moon.

SUNSET SPRITZ

PIER BAR
II HICKSON RD, DAWES POINT

Pier Bar sits almost under the Sydney Harbour Bridge and its waterside vantage point is made all the more special by the iconic sunsets. Bar manager Gavin Conor says the views as the sun is setting over the water inspired the Sunset Spritz and he suggests sipping it at the correct time of day to fully soak up the experience. Pier Bar partners with Kings Cross Distillery, from the nearby suburb of Kings Cross, for this signature cocktail.

GLASSWARE: Wineglass
GARNISH: Orange peel disk

- 2 oz. | 60 ml orange juice
- ½ oz. | 15 ml Raspberry Syrup (see recipe)
- 1⅓ oz. | 40 ml gin
- ½ oz. | 15 ml falernum syrup
- Soda water, to top

1. Stir all of the ingredients, except for the soda, together in a mixing glass.

2. Pour the cocktail over ice and top with soda and garnish with an orange peel disk.

RASPBERRY SYRUP: In a small saucepan over medium heat, combine 1 cup raspberries, 1 cup water, 1 cup sugar, and 2 tablespoons fresh lemon juice and stir until the sugar is dissolved. Remove the mixture from heat and muddle the raspberries to release their juices. Allow the syrup to cool then strain it before use.

MENZIES BAR DIRTY GIN MARTINI

Prior to its redevelopment, Shell House was home to the Menzies Hotel, and the Menzies Bar aims to mix history, hospitality, and good times. According to owner Brett Robinson, a daily Martini hour quickly earned Menzies Bar a following as the home of the Martini in Sydney.

GLASSWARE: Martini glass
GARNISH: Green olives on a skewer

- 1⅓ oz. | 40 ml Tanqueray London Dry Gin
- ⅓ oz. | 10 ml olive brine

1. Chill a martini glass in the freezer. Combine the gin and olive brine with ice in a mixing glass.

2. Stir and strain the cocktail into the chilled martini glass straight from the freezer.

3. Garnish with green olives on a skewer.

MANGO MEZCAL TOMMY'S

BOPP & TONE
60 CARRINGTON ST, SYDNEY

A Tommy's Margarita is already a much-loved cocktail at Bopp & Tone. Pairing it with Australia's Kensington Pride mangoes elevates the drink to a new level and evokes lying on Bondi Beach in the sun with its smokey, citrus, sweet, and fruity elements. The perfection is in the process, says bar manager Donovan Binks. "It's essential when we sous vide the ingredients to have as much of those delicious fibers infuse with the mezcal," he says. This not only enriches the cocktail with flavor, but also gives it a bright yellow hue.

GLASSWARE: Rocks glass

- 1¾ oz. | 50 ml mango-infused mezcal
- 1 oz. | 30 ml fresh lime juice
- ½ oz. | 15 ml agave syrup
- Fresh lime juice, for the rim
- Tajín, for the rim

1. Add all of the ingredients to a cocktail shaker and shake.

2. Dip a rocks glass in lime juice and sprinkle the glass generously with Tajín.

3. Strain the cocktail into the rocks glass and serve.

NEGATIVE GEARING

CLOCKTOWER BAR
SHELL HOUSE, 37 MARGARET ST, SYDNEY

S hell House is historically significant as the only surviving interwar commercial palazzo-style building in Sydney, clad with glazed terracotta "faience" blocks. Standing at 214 feet (65.5 meters) high, Shell House's façade is also one of the tallest retained heritage façades in the world. The Clocktower Bar, on level 9, is housed within the building's iconic 400-ton clock. Negative Gearing is a playful and tongue-in-cheek reference to real estate investing, a never-ending topic of conversation in Sydney.

GLASSWARE: Rocks glass
GARNISH: Pandan leaf, grated nutmeg

- 1 oz. | 30 ml Rittenhouse Straight Rye 100
- ⅚ oz. | 25 ml White Chocolate-and-Hazelnut-Washed Bourbon (see recipe)
- ⅕ oz. | 6.25 ml Mr Black Cold Brew Coffee Liqueur
- 1 teaspoon | 5 ml kithul
- ¹⁄₁₀ oz. | 3.5 ml banana oleo
- ⅛ oz. | 2.5 ml Popcorn Bulleit Bourbon (see recipe)
- ¹⁄₂₄ oz. | 1.25 ml Fernet-Branca

1. Combine all of the ingredients in a mixing glass.

2. Stir and pour the cocktail into a rocks glass filled with quality ice cubes.

3. Garnish with a pandan leaf and grated nutmeg.

WHITE CHOCOLATE-AND-HAZELNUT-WASHED BOURBON:
Sous vide white chocolate ice cream and hazelnut ice cream into 1 bottle of Bulleit Bourbon, then place it in the freezer. Drip-thaw the bourbon through cheesecloth—this makes the liquid clear, resulting in a velvety mouthfeel infused with the unctuous, delicious flavors of the white chocolate and hazelnut with the backdrop of fresh cream. This process takes 2 days.

POPCORN BULLEIT BOURBON: Add sweet and salty, good-quality popcorn to 1 bottle of Bulleit Bourbon and let it infuse for 3 hours, then strain it. The bourbon takes on all the oily goodness and popcorn flavor during the infusion.

LOVE OVER MONEY

SKY BAR
SHELL HOUSE, 37 MARGARET ST, SYDNEY

A s its name suggests, sipping a cocktail at Sky Bar is like having a cocktail in the sky. Guests have an amazing view of the Sydney skyline and when the floor-to-ceiling glass doors retract, they can enjoy their libations in the fresh air. Love Over Money carries the spirit of Venice to its Sydney home and is inspired by the Tintoretto by Guiseppe Capriani of Harry's Bar fame. It has the warming spice of pink peppercorn and ginger. Pomegranate and lemon make it zippy and refreshing, Prosecco is added for fizz, while nuances of rose water and muscat tie it together. Temperature is the key to a successful cocktail. Everything should be chilled—soda, mixers, water, and guests.

GLASSWARE: Wineglass
GARNISH: Mint sprig, lemon slice

- ¼ oz. | 7.5 ml pink peppercorn infused–Tanqueray London Dry Gin

- ⅖ oz. | 12.5 ml Tanqueray London Dry Gin

- ⅛ oz. | 3.75 ml Ginger Syrup (see recipe)

- 1 teaspoon | 5 ml Monin Pomegranate Syrup

- ⅔ oz. | 20 ml verjus

- 1⁄25 oz. | 1.25 ml apple cider vinegar

- 1⁄125 oz. | 0.25 ml Pernod

- 1⁄125 oz. | 0.25 ml rose water

- 2 oz. | 60 ml Bandini Prosecco

1. Fill a wineglass with ice cubes.

2. Build your drink directly into the glass by adding the gin, ginger, pomegranate syrup, verjus, apple cider vinegar, Pernod, and rose water.

3. Add the prosecco as the last liquid.

4. Garnish the drink with a mint sprig and lemon slice.

GINGER SYRUP: In a saucepan on medium heat, combine 1 cup granulated sugar and ¾ cup water. Stir constantly until the sugar is dissolved. Add 1 cup sliced fresh ginger, peeled, and continue to heat, bringing the syrup to a light boil. Cover, reduce the heat, and allow the syrup to simmer for about 15 minutes. Remove the pan from heat and allow the syrup to cool and steep in the covered pan for about 1 hour, or until it reaches your preferred taste. Strain out the ginger and bottle under a tight seal.

TROPICAL COFFEE MARGARITA

Venue manager Sarah Proietti says the attention to detail in crafting each drink, along with the expertise of Maybe Sammy's bartenders and the theatrical approach of service, ensures a memorable experience for guests. The Tropical Coffee Margarita brings together the city's love for both coffee and cocktails. At the heart of the drink is Mr Black Cold Brew Coffee Liqueur, a high-quality coffee liqueur produced in Australia that has garnered a cult following globally.

GLASSWARE: Double rocks glass

- Salt, for the rim
- 1 oz. | 30 ml blanco tequila
- 1 oz. | 30 ml Mr Black Cold Brew Coffee Liqueur
- 1 oz. | 30 ml Mango Syrup (see recipe)
- ⅔ oz. | 20 ml fresh lime juice

1. Add a salt rim to a double rocks glass.

2. Mix together the remaining ingredients in a shaker with plenty of ice.

3. Shake the drink vigorously to achieve the ideal dilution and temperature.

4. Strain the cocktail over ice and serve.

MANGO SYRUP: Mix together equal parts sugar and mango puree until the sugar completely dissolves. It should have a smooth and balanced sweetness.

DEAN & NANCY

2 HUNTER ST, SYDNEY

Add a dose of decadence and a dash of drama, serve with precision and fun, and you are at Dean & Nancy, a cocktail bar in the A by Adina Sydney.

"We've been wanting to do this for a while—to bring the magic of a 1950s-style 'hotel bar' experience from Maybe Sammy into a premium hotel," says Maybe Sammy founder Stefano Catino of the creative partnership with A by Adina. "Our guests' happiness is our top priority. Yes, we have a lot of fun, but we prepare for that. We are very detail-oriented; nothing is overlooked. Once guests arrive at Dean & Nancy, we want to float around the room and make sure everyone is happy."

The drama of the 360-degree twinkling city views is not lost on guests, nor is the experience.

23RD & BROADWAY

DEAN & NANCY
2 HUNTER ST, SYDNEY

The 23rd & Broadway was on the first cocktail menu at Dean & Nancy and represents Sydney's restaurant scene, in particular its famous steak houses such as Firedoor in Surry Hills. "We wanted to recreate a steak house feel, with roasted macadamias, rye whisky, fortified wine, and native Australian sandalwood syrup," says Dean & Nancy restaurant and bar manager Stefano Filardi. "With this scenography effect and representation, we add the incense as a garnish element to smoke the glass and transport you to a classic, elegant steak house."

GLASSWARE: Rocks glass or earthenware cup

- 1¾ oz. | 50 ml rye whiskey infused with toasted macadamia nuts
- ⅓ oz. | 10 ml Madeira
- 1 teaspoon | 5 ml sandalwood syrup

1. Freeze a rocks glass or earthenware cup. Stir all of the ingredients together with ice in a mixing glass.

2. Smoke a frozen glass with a lit incense stick.

3. Strain the ingredients into the smoked glass.

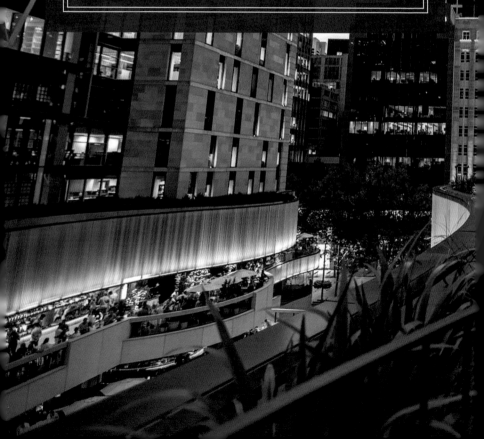

ROOFTOP ON BOTSWANA BUTCHERY

19-29 MARTIN PL, SYDNEY

Nestled within Sydney's ornate heritage buildings and dramatic skyscrapers, Rooftop on Botswana Butchery is a relative newcomer to the city's bar scene. However, it has quickly become a favorite destination for after-work drinks, late evening tipples, and everything in between.

SUMMERTIME

ROOFTOP ON BOTSWANA BUTCHERY
19-29 MARTIN PL, SYDNEY

The al fresco spirit of Rooftop on Botswana Butchery is expertly encapsulated by its Summertime cocktail, which features craft gin, limoncello, and hibiscus syrup. While the bar uses a gin from the rainforest hinterland of Byron Bay, any dry craft gin will suit. Summertime is the ideal drink to sip and enjoy under the summer sun. To ensure the perfect serve, use a fine strain to achieve a foaming effect when double straining. Using fresh basil as a garnish gives the cocktail a vibrant, herbaceous aroma.

GLASSWARE: Coupe glass
GARNISH: Basil leaf

- 1½ oz. | 45 ml Brookies Byron Dry Gin
- ⅔ oz. | 20 ml Manly Spirits Zesty Limoncello
- ½ oz. | 15 ml hibiscus syrup
- ½ oz. | 15 ml fresh lemon juice
- ⅓ oz. | 10 ml basil syrup

1. Combine all of the ingredients in a cocktail shaker and shake with ice.

2. Double-strain into a coupe glass.

3. Garnish with a basil leaf.

SYDNEY G&T

ARIA
1 MACQUARIE ST, SYDNEY

Aria has been an icon of Sydney's food and dining scene since 1999 and its panoramic views of the Sydney Harbour Bridge and Sydney Opera House set the stage to wow locals and visitors, day and night. To make the perfect Sydney G&T, it's important to follow the recipe. It also helps to know what the terms mean. Shaking and stirring, for instance, are different methods . . . as a certain British spy would attest.

GLASSWARE: Rocks glass

GARNISH: Tasmanian Pepperberry Glass (see recipe)

- 2½ oz. | 75 ml Quince Gin (see recipe)
- 2 to 3 drops Pimento Tincture (see recipe)
- Indian tonic water, to top

1. Pour the gin and pimento tincture over ice in a rocks glass.

2. Top with Indian tonic water.

3. Garnish with Tasmanian pepperberry glass.

QUINCE GIN: Put 2 lbs. 3¼ oz. (1 kg) quince, peeled and chopped into quarters; 23 oz. (700 ml) gin; 5⅓ oz. (150 grams) honey; 4 to 5 pieces whole star anise; and ⅒ oz. (3 grams) Tasmanian pepperberry in a vacuum-sealed bag. Sous vide at 133°F (56°C) for at least 8 hours. Let it cool, then filter the gin through a coffee filter and bottle it.

PIMENTO TINCTURE: Vacuum-seal 3 ½ oz. (100 grams) pimento berries and 6⅔ oz. (200 ml) everclear (60% ABV). Sous vide at 133°F (56°C) for 5 to 6 hours. Let the mixture cool, then filter the tincture through a coffee filter and bottle it.

TASMANIAN PEPPERBERRY GLASS: Combine equal parts iso-malt and glucose and cook them together with Tasmanian pepperberry. Allow the mixture to cool. Crack the "glass" into shapes.

BELLY DANCER

BAHARAT
100 BARANGAROO AVE, BARANGAROO

According to Baharat bartender Emre Bilgin, cocktails at home often don't taste the same as those served at bars and restaurants because the design, lighting, music, and even the sound of cocktail shakers are different. Without the ambience of the bar, you must concentrate on good ingredients to make a great cocktail at home. Another must is high-quality ice. Emre suggests choosing large ice cubes to ensure the desired dilution.

GLASSWARE: Coupe glass

- 1½ oz. | 45 ml mezcal
- 1 oz. | 30 ml Allspice Dram (see recipe)
- ⅓ oz. | 10 ml raki
- 1 oz. | 30 ml acid-adjusted grapefruit juice
- Sunflower Seed Dust (see recipe), for the rim

1. Add all of the liquid ingredients to a cocktail shaker with ice and shake well.

2. Serve with salted sunflower seed dust on the rim of the glass.

SUNFLOWER SEED DUST: Add a pinch of Maldon sea salt flakes and a pinch of raw sunflower seeds to a spice grinder and process the mixture into a fine powder.

ALLSPICE DRAM: Combine 25⅓ oz. (750 ml) dark rum, ⅙ oz. (5 grams) ground cloves, 1 cinnamon stick, and 1¾ oz. (50 grams) allspice in a container. Let the spice mix infuse the rumor 2 days. Strain the mixture, then add 8 ½ oz. (250 ml) simple syrup.

FIRESTONE

CIRQ
CROWN SYDNEY, LEVEL 26/1 BARANGAROO AVE,
BARANGAROO

Firestone is dark and seductive, yet confidently understated at first glance, with a warm undertone that really shines when hit with some light. Using a cognac that you really enjoy makes a difference with this cocktail (which calls for Martell VS). Marionette Dry Cassis gives a great cassis taste without imparting a sticky mouthfeel or lingering too long, but this balance can be lost if too much dilution occurs. Stop stirring the drink just before perfect dilution and serve it with a big, clear ice cube to leave any further dilution up to personal preference.

GLASSWARE: Coupe glass

GARNISH: Wheel of candied cayenne pepper

- 1 oz. | 30 ml Martell VS
- ½ oz. | 15 ml Marionette Dry Cassis
- ½ oz. | 15 ml crème de cacao
- 1 teaspoon | 5 ml spicy cayenne syrup
- 2 dashes Bittermens Xocolatl Mole Bitters

1. Build the cocktail in a mixing glass by adding the cognac, cassis, crème de cacao, spicy cayenne syrup, and bitters.

2. Stir the ingredients together, making sure not to overdilute.

3. Strain and serve the cocktail with a big ice cube and a sliver of candied cayenne pepper.

DRAGON FIRE

TEAHOUSE
CROWN SYDNEY, LEVEL 3/1 BARANGAROO AVE,
BARANGAROO

The Dragon Fire is the perfect demonstration of how different traditions and flavors have influenced Sydney's cocktail scene. At Teahouse, beauty and luxury are mixed with spiciness to create a venue that resembles an Asian palace. A riff on a Spicy Margarita, the Dragon Fire has strong umami and savory flavors. The top of the glass must be clean for the bubble to sit firm. If you have a smoking gun (like a Flavour Blaster Mini), you can make this cocktail extra elegant with a smoke bubble garnish.

GLASSWARE: Wineglass

- XO sauce, for the rim
- Salt, for the rim
- 2 oz. | 60 ml Chile-and-Coriander-Infused Tequila (see recipe)
- 1 oz. | 30 ml fresh lime juice
- ½ oz. | 15 ml agave syrup

1. Wet the rim of a wineglass then dip the glass rim into crumbs of XO sauce and salt.

2. Shake the remaining ingredients together in a cocktail shaker.

3. Pour the cocktail into the rimmed glass.

CHILE-AND-CILANTRO-INFUSED TEQUILA:
Add 3 to 4 stalks of cilantro, chopped and 2 bird's
eye chile peppers, chopped, to a bottle (700 ml) of
Tequila Herradura Silver. Let the ingredients infuse
for at least 24 hours.

ELOPE IN A TUXEDO

BAR 83
LEVEL 4/108 MARKET ST, SYDNEY

High above Sydney—83 stories above street level—Bar 83 sits in the iconic Sydney Tower. With floor-to-ceiling windows and nods to nostalgia, guests can revel in a 260-degree view of the Sydney cityscape. The Elope in a Tuxedo was inspired during Sydney World-Pride by conversations among many international couples about eloping to Amsterdam, when the Netherlands was announced as the first country to legalize same sex marriage in 2001.

GLASSWARE: Nick & Nora glass

GARNISH: 2 dashes Peychaud's bitters

- 1½ oz. | 45 ml Archie Rose Straight Dry Gin
- ½ oz. | 30 ml fresh lemon juice
- Pinch flaky sea salt
- 1 teaspoon | 5 ml Luxardo Maraschino Originale
- ⅓ oz. | 10 ml Cello Dolce Melone

1. Add all of the ingredients to a cocktail shaker and hard-shake.

2. Fine-strain the cocktail into a Nick & Nora glass.

3. Garnish with crossed lines of the bitters.

KYOTO ROSE

REIGN CHAMPAGNE PARLOUR & BAR
LEVEL 1 SHOP 48/455 GEORGE ST, SYDNEY

R eign Champagne Parlour & Bar is located in the beautiful Queen Victoria Building in the heart of Sydney's CBD. The building opened in 1898 and was named the year before it opened by the Sydney Council to mark "the unprecedented and glorious reign of her majesty the Queen." Reign continues the tradition of honoring Queen Victoria, while offering shoppers, visitors, and the day-to-day foot traffic an escape into luxury. The Kyoto Rose has a distinctly Sydney flavor by using gin produced at Poor Toms Distillery in the inner western suburb of Marrickville.

GLASSWARE: Nick & Nora glass

GARNISH: Rose petal

- 1½ oz. | 45 ml Poor Toms Strawberry Gin
- ⅓ oz. | 10 ml St-Germain Elderflower Liqueur
- 1 teaspoon | 5 ml Campari

- ⅓ oz. | 10 ml lychee syrup
- ½ oz. | 15 ml rose syrup
- ⅓ oz. | 10 ml fresh lime juice

1. Add all of the ingredients to a cocktail shaker with ice.

2. Shake and fine-strain the cocktail into a Nick & Nora glass.

3. Garnish with a single rose petal.

GREAT ESCAPE

BOTANIC HOUSE
I MRS MACQUARIES RD, SYDNEY

In the heart of the heritage-listed 74-acre (30-hectare) Royal Botanic Gardens, Botanic House by Luke Nguyen attracts locals and visitors in droves. The sorbet in the Great Escape takes this cocktail from good to great.

GLASSWARE: Highball glass

GARNISH: Pineapple wedge, diced pickled mango

- 1½ oz. | 45 ml Pampero Aniversario Rum
- 1½ oz. | 45 ml pineapple juice
- ½ oz. | 15 ml black cardamom syrup
- 3½ oz. | 100 grams coconut-and-lychee sorbet, plus more to top
- 1 oz. | 30 ml Fever-Tree Sparkling Lime & Yuzu Soda

1. Combine all of the ingredients, except for the soda water and garnishes, in a cocktail shaker.

2. Shake hard and strain the cocktail into a highball over ice.

3. Top with the soda and add half a scoop of sorbet.

4. Garnish with a pineapple wedge and a piece of diced pickled mango.

ARCHIE SAZERAC

ESQ BAR
LEVEL 2/455 GEORGE ST, SYDNEY

Located in the beautiful and historic Queen Victoria Building, ESQ Bar & Dining is a Prohibition-themed speakeasy. Use a silicone mold for the ice to ensure a clean square block.

GLASSWARE: Large rocks glass
GARNISH: Snapped lemon myrtle leaf, twist of orange peel

- ⅓ oz. | 10 ml La Fée Parisienne Absinthe Supérieure
- 2 dashes Peychaud's bitters
- ⅓ oz. | 10 ml Wattleseed Syrup (see recipe)
- 1¾ oz. | 50 ml Archie Rose Rye Malt Whisky

1. In a shaker, wash ice with the absinthe and add the bitters, syrup, and whiskey.

2. Strain the cocktail over a block of ice into a large rocks glass.

3. Garnish with a snapped lemon myrtle leaf and twist of orange peel.

WATTLESEED SYRUP: In a small saucepan over medium heat, combine 1 cup water, 1 cup superfine (caster) sugar, ¾ cup brown sugar, 1 tablespoon (20 grams) ground wattleseed, and ¼ teaspoon salt and bring the mixture to a simmer for about 30 minutes, stirring until the sugar is dissolved. Allow the syrup to cool before using.

FLYING FISH

SARDINE BAR
LEVEL 8/25 MARTIN PL, SYDNEY

Funky cocktails, upbeat music, and its very own dedicated dumpling chef make Sardine Bar one of the grooviest bars in Sydney. The bar is co-located with White + Wong's restaurant in the heart of the city. The Flying Fish is named for the Australian flying fish, which is found off the coast of NSW.

GLASSWARE: Highball glass

GARNISH: Dehydrated lime slice

- 1½ oz. | 45 ml Archie Rose Signature Dry Gin
- 1 oz. | 30 ml apple juice
- ⅓ oz. | 10 ml fresh lime juice
- ½ oz. | 15 ml G.E. Massenez Green Apple Liqueur
- Red Bull Green Edition, to top

1. In a cocktail shaker, shake all of the ingredients, except for the Red Bull, together.

2. Pour the cocktail into a highball.

3. Invigorate the flavors with a generous top-up of the Red Bull.

4. Garnish with a dehydrated lime slice.

RHUBARBIE

THE LOFT
3 LIME ST, SYDNEY

Nothing says Sydney like drawing tastes from lots of different corners of the world, says assistant venue manager Sean Gill. "We combined Venezuelan and Jamaican rum as well as the classic English dessert, apple and rhubarb crumble, for a perfectly balanced cocktail to enjoy on a night out," he says. The secret to serving a cocktail perfectly are the two P's, according to Gill: preparation and personality. The first P (preparation) is ensuring all your glassware, syrups, spirits, and garnishes are ready to go so it is a smooth and efficient process. The second P (personality) is bringing the X factor: it's the unique and interesting bartender who turns a good drink into a great experience.

GLASSWARE: Coupette glass
GARNISH: Crushed Scotch finger biscuits (or shortbread),
½ oz. | 15 ml aquafaba or egg white

- 1½ oz. | 45 ml Apple and Rhubarb Syrup (see recipe)
- ⅓ oz. | 10 ml fresh pink grapefruit juice
- 1 oz. | 30 ml Pampero Especial Rum
- 1 oz. | 30 ml Appleton Estate Signature Jamaica Rum

1. Chill a coupette glass. In a cocktail shaker, dry-shake all of the ingredients without ice.

2. Add ice and shake.

3. Double-strain the cocktail into the chilled coupette.

4. Top with aquafaba foam, then sprinkle over crushed Scotch finger biscuits.

APPLE AND RHUBARB SYRUP: Combine diced apples and rhubarb and simmer with equal parts sugar and water until the syrup is a deep, rich red and the fruits are soft. Strain the syrup before using.

LOST IN PARADISE

THE ROOK
LEVEL 7/56-58 YORK ST, SYDNEY

The Rook offers a sanctuary above the hustle and bustle of the city where you can immerse yourself in its carefully curated cocktail list. Venue manager Sarah Riahi says Sydneysiders are "just busy people," all yearning for the vacation that always seems to be just out of reach. This was the inspiration for Lost in Paradise—to create a drink where reality fades away and your tastebuds embark on a delightful adventure, transporting you to a world of sun-kissed beaches and swaying palm trees. For the rum, The Rook uses Bati, but any would work.

GLASSWARE: Highball glass
GARNISH: Orange wedge, mint sprig, dehydrated lime slice, edible flower

- 1½ oz. | 45 ml pineapple juice
- 1½ oz. | 45 ml cranberry juice
- 1 oz. | 30 ml Bati White Rum
- ⅔ oz. | 20 ml fresh lime juice
- ½ oz. | 15 ml Cointreau
- ⅓ oz. | 10 ml falernum

1. Combine all of the ingredients in a cocktail shaker.

2. Top with ice and shake.

3. Strain the cocktail into a highball and add the garnishes.

THE GHOST OF PIÑA

GOWINGS BAR AT QT SYDNEY
49 MARKET ST, SYDNEY

Gowings, a men's clothing store established in Sydney in 1868, was a much-loved institution until it closed in 2006. Now, the rich history of the building infuses Gowings Bar at QT Sydney. The Ghost of Piña cocktail evokes a sense of the unexpected. According to food and beverage director Jeremy Metzroth, the cocktail, an adaptation of the Piña Colada, has been a favorite since its debut in December 2022.

GLASSWARE: Rocks glass
GARNISH: Pineapple leaf, cherry

- 1½ oz. | 45 ml Appleton Estate Signature Jamaica Rum
- 1⅓ oz. | 40 ml pineapple juice
- 1⅕ oz. | 35 ml coconut syrup

- 1 oz. | 30 ml coconut water
- ⅔ oz. | 20 ml coconut syrup
- ½ oz. | 15 ml Malibu Original
- ½ oz. | 15 ml fresh lime juice

1. Mix all of the ingredients together and allow the mixture to rest in the fridge for up to 30 minutes.

2. Line a strainer with cheesecloth and set the strainer over a bowl.

3. Pour the batch from the fridge over the cheesecloth so the clear liquid can steep through.

4. Repeat the process until the liquid is clear.

5. Discard any leftovers in the cheesecloth.

6. Serve in a rocks glass with a large ice cube.

7. Garnish with a pineapple leaf and a cherry.

8. The batch can be served immediately or refrigerated for up to 5 days.

GRAPES 'N' GRAPPA

EAU DE VIE
WYNYARD LANE, 285 GEORGE ST, SYDNEY

Eau de Vie is a 1920s-influenced bar with moody lighting, glass cabinets, leather seats, and a legendary list of craft cocktails. Much like the unassuming but vibrant cocktail scene in Sydney, this floral wet Martini riff offers more than meets than eye.

GLASSWARE: Coupetini glass

GARNISH: Lemon disk, 3 pickled red grapes

- 1⅓ oz. | 40 ml Cacao Butter–Washed Absolut Elyx (see recipe)
- ⅔ oz. | 20 ml Unico Pomelo Dry White Vermouth
- ⅙ oz. | 5 ml Joseph Cartron White Cacao Liqueur
- ¹⁄₃₂ oz. | 1 ml saline solution
- ¼ oz. | 7.5 ml Nonino Il Moscato Grappa

1. Add all of the ingredients to a mixing glass with cubed ice.

2. Stir until your preferred dilution is achieved and the drink is well chilled, then pour the cocktail into a coupetini.

3. Twist a lemon disk over the drink to express its oils then add the disk as garnish, along with 3 pickled red grapes on a skewer.

CACAO BUTTER–WASHED ABSOLUT ELYX: In a small saucepan over low heat, melt 1 oz. (30 grams) cacao butter then remove the pan from heat. Add 1 (750 ml) bottle of Absolut Elyx and allow the mixture to rest at room temperature for 30 minutes. Freeze the mixture overnight then strain the vodka through cheesecloth or a coffee filter. Keep the cacao butter: it can be reused to wash vodka.

MINI DRY MARTINI

BAR TOPA
4 PALINGS LANE, SYDNEY

Positioned in cozy Palings Lane, Bar Topa's name is derived from the Spanish word *topar*, meaning to "come across" for some tapas and pintxos before the next stop. The bar has a focus on delivering aperitifs and mini cocktails with Spanish flair. With the "mini movement" in full swing in Sydney, the drink is very much in vogue for cocktail fans.

GLASSWARE: Mini martini glass
GARNISH: Lemon twist, olive, or both

- 2 oz. | 60 ml Absolut Elyx
- 1 oz. | 10 ml Madeira
- 1 oz. | 10 ml filtered water

1. Chill a mini martini glass in the freezer. Stir all of the ingredients together in a mixing glass and place the mixture in the freezer for 2 hours.

2. Pour the cocktail into the frozen mini martini glass and garnish with a lemon twist or olive or both.

SECRETS OF ALEJA

CARDEA
300 BARANGAROO AVE, BARANGAROO

Nestled in the heart of Barangaroo, Cardea takes its name from the Roman goddess Cardea, who fearlessly guards doorways against evil spirits. The intimate haven is adorned with elegant vintage furniture, luxurious velvet interiors, and private booths that exude the charm of a clandestine speakeasy. "Sydney's vibe is super laidback and refreshing, which is exactly what this cocktail emulates," master mixologist George Bekarian says. "It's invigorating—soft notes of gin infused with fragrant ginger and rhubarb give off a balmy, summery feel. We add cherry jam that comes locally sourced and mesh these elements together to create a cocktail that is the perfect balance of sweet and sour on the palate—sophisticated yet relaxed, like Sydney."

GLASSWARE: Coupette glass

GARNISH: Star anise pod

- 1½ oz. | 45 ml gin infused with ginger and rhubarb
- ⅚ oz. | 25 ml fresh lime juice
- Barspoon cherry jam
- 3 dashes cherry bitters
- ½ oz. | 15 ml egg whites or 2 drops of cocktail foam

1. Chill a coupette glass. Pour the gin into a cocktail shaker, then add the remaining ingredients.

2. Dry-shake for 30 seconds.

3. Shake with ice for 30 seconds.

4. Double-strain the cocktail into the chilled coupette and garnish with a star anise pod.

MORRIS MANHATTAN

The Morris Manhattan highlights the rich oaky flavors of Morris Australian Single Malt Whisky Tokay Barrel and its fortified wine counterpart, Morris of Rutherglen Cellar Reserve Grand Topaque. Together, they make for a perfect evening aperitif. You can substitute your favorite tokay barrel–aged whiskey. If you can't get hold of the Topaque wine, use any fortified red wine.

GLASSWARE: Coupetini glass
GARNISH: Maraschino cherry

- 2 oz.| 60 ml Morris Australian Single Malt Whisky Tokay Barrel
- ⅔ oz. | 20 ml rosso vermouth
- ⅓ oz. | 10 ml Morris of Rutherglen Cellar Reserve Grand Topaque
- Bitters, to taste
- Orange peel

1. Add all of the ingredients to a mixing glass with ice and stir until well chilled. Strain the cocktail into a coupetini.

2. Twist the orange peel to release its essential oils and discard the peel.

3. Garnish with a maraschino cherry and serve.

GOLD RUSH

BRIDGE LANE
6 BRIDGE LANE, SYDNEY

Traditionally made with bourbon, Morris Whisky's take on the Gold Rush brings an added sweetness to the mix from the spirit's time in fortified wine barrels. The whiskey displays intense flavors of toffee, mocha, and soft caramel that perfectly complement the lemon juice and honey to create a drink that is intensely palatable.

GLASSWARE: Rocks glass

GARNISH: Pear wedge

- **2 oz. | 60 ml Morris Australian Single Malt Whisky Tokay Barrel**
- **1 oz. | 30 ml fresh lemon juice**

- **⅔ oz. | 20 ml Honey Ginger Syrup (see recipe)**

1. Add all of the ingredients to a cocktail shaker with ice.

2. Shake for 10 to 15 seconds, then strain into a rocks glass.

HONEY GINGER SYRUP: Bring 5 oz. (150 ml) water and 1 oz. (30 grams) fresh ginger, peeled and diced, to a boil. Mix in 10 oz. (300 ml) honey. Let the mixture cool and then strain the syrup.

MORRIS

RUTHERGLEN

AUSTRALIAN
SINGLE MALT WHISKY

**TOKAY
BARREL**

MORRIS HIGHBALL

BRIDGE LANE
6 BRIDGE LANE, SYDNEY

For this take on a classic Highball, you can substitute your favorite single malt whiskey if you can't source Morris of Rutherglen's fabulous single malt.

GLASSWARE: Highball glass

GARNISH: Orange wedge

- 1½ oz. | 45 ml Morris Australian Single Malt Signature Whisky
- ½ oz. | 15 ml orange curaçao

- 1 teaspoon | 5 ml 2:1 simple syrup
- Soda water, to top

1. Build the cocktail in a highball glass and top with soda.

2. Garnish with an orange wedge.

QUEEN MARGIE

CAFFE Q'S
R2002/50 BRIDGE ST, SYDNEY

The Queen Margie was created by owner Quynh Nguyen for National Tequila Day. Nguyen is globally renowned for his drinks consultancy and creative bar menus at locations such as Toko Dubai, Tanjong Beach Club Singapore, Intercontinental Golf and Spa Resort Fiji, plus top Sydney restaurants Margaret, Icebergs, and Fred's.

GLASSWARE: Double rocks glass
GARNISH: Lime wedge

- 1⅓ oz. | 40 ml reposado tequila
- 1 oz. | 30 ml fresh lime juice
- ½ oz. | 15 ml agave beer
- ½ oz. | 15 ml Dubonnet Rouge Grand Aperitif de France
- 3 dashes rhubarb bitters

1. Freeze a double rocks glass. In a cocktail shaker, quick-shake all of the ingredients.

2. Pour the cocktail into an ice-cold double rocks glass.

3. Garnish with a lime wedge.

BOARD GA
AVAILABL
AT THE BA

YCK LANEWAYS

SWEET EMOTION

LOCK, STOCK & BARRELLED

THE LITTLE GRACE

FARMER'S MARKET

MANGO WEISSY MARTINI

FUEGO DE ESTEBAN

THE CHARLES MARTINI

BENEATH THE SHEETS

EXTRA! EXTRA!

AFRICOLA

TENNESSEE TRUCK STOP

BARBER SHOP GIMLET

ESPRESSO MARTINI

Hidden within Sydney's CBD (central business district) you will find a buzzing bar precinct dubbed YCK Laneways, which spans across York, Clarence, and Kent Streets (hence YCK).

YCK Laneways was established by a collective of small bar owners in 2021, with the aim of inspiring Sydneysiders to rediscover the city and to inject some much needed vibrance back into the CBD. According to YCK Laneways Association vice president, Karl Schlothauer, who owns the New York–inspired Stitch Bar, bars in the precinct are predominantly located in older-style buildings, with the uniqueness of each space adding to its character.

"Whether it is a bar tucked away at the end of a laneway, or simply a door that leads you down to a basement bar, I don't think there is anywhere else in the world that has such a high concentration of world-class venues in such a small footprint," he says.

KARL SCHLOTHAUER, STITCH BAR

Stitch Bar is hidden behind a faux seamstress, down a grand staircase. When you enter the basement bar you will find a drinking den where you can enjoy a rare whiskey or a cutting-edge cocktail while eating American diner–style food.

A few steps away you will find bars ranging from the upmarket Mexican Esteban to the British-style pub The Duke of Clarence. Schlothauer is proud of the camaraderie that exists between all the venues, staff, and owners in YCK Laneways. They lend each other stock on busy Friday nights, share trade secrets, and happily suggest the next venue for bar-hopping guests to visit within the precinct.

"The amount of creativity YCK allows us is truly limitless," Karl explains. "Recently, it has opened doors to various collaboration opportunities, such as working with celebrity chefs, regional producers, emerging performing artists, and even different levels of government. There is a whole world of weird and wonderful things and people that I find fascinating in YCK, and all of them contribute to creating exceptional experiences for our guests."

SWEET EMOTION

STITCH BAR
61 YORK ST, SYDNEY

The Sweet Emotion takes inspiration from Sydney's love of coffee and sophisticated nightlife. It is a drink created as an after-dinner treat, something to indulge in after a beautiful meal. Bartender Cristiano Beretta says it is a nightcap with a dessert kind of feeling. "The perfect serve combines a few different factors," Cristiano says, "the right glassware, the ice, the balance of the ingredients, the garnish. The aesthetic of the drink as a whole is what creates a perfect serve."

GLASSWARE: Old-fashioned glass

GARNISH: Coffee Air (see recipe), chocolate truffle

- 1 oz. | 30 ml Woodford Reserve Straight Bourbon Whiskey
- ⅔ oz. | 20 ml Giffard Banane du Bresil
- ⅓ oz. | 10 ml demerara simple syrup
- 3 drops Abbott's Aromatic Bitters

1. Combine all of the ingredients in a mixing glass and stir.

2. Strain into an old-fashioned glass over a big ice cube and garnish with coffee air and a chocolate truffle.

COFFEE AIR. In a jar, add 3 oz. (90 ml) of cold brew coffee and 2 pinches of lecithin. Submerge an aerator stone in the liquid and turn the aerator on. When this forms bigger bubbles, scoop off the amount needed and place it on the drink.

LOCK, STOCK & BARRELLED

THE DUKE OF CLARENCE
156 CLARENCE ST, SYDNEY

Hidden in the heart of the city, The Duke of Clarence is an eighteenth-century London–inspired tavern dedicated to cocktails, cask ale, and British eats. "We get a great collection of expats in who come in looking for a Scotch egg or Sunday roast that'll take them back to a time across the ocean," says venue manager Tom Joseph. "We also get a lot of locals who've spent time over in London or Edinburgh or Belfast and are coming in to raise a glass to friends far away." The bar bulk-builds its Lock, Stock & Barrelled and ages it in an American oak barrel for a few weeks before stirring it down and serving it. "If you don't have a barrel available, it still tastes fantastic when you make it fresh," Joseph says.

GLASSWARE: Nick & Nora glass

GARNISH: Lemon twist

- 1 oz. | 30 ml blanco tequila
- ⅔ oz. | 20 ml sweet vermouth
- ⅓ oz. | 10 ml Amaro Nonino Quintessentia
- 1 teaspoon | 5 ml Yellow Chartreuse
- 2 dashes chocolate bitters
- 2 dashes barrel-aged bitters

1. Combine all of the ingredients in a mixing glass, add ice, and stir until well diluted to soften the flavors, about 20 to 30 seconds.
2. Strain the cocktail into a Nick & Nora or other stemmed cocktail glass and garnish with a twist of lemon.

THE LITTLE GRACE

SINCE I LEFT YOU
338 KENT ST, SYDNEY

The Little Grace was named in honor of the first regulars at Since I Left You. Andrew and Ebru lived across the road from the bar and every week they would visit with a new group of friends to show it off. Owner Nick White says this was really comforting and showed the sense of community that exists in Sydney CBD. "When they became pregnant, we promised them we would name a drink after their child," Nick says. Ever since their daughter, Grace, was born eleven years ago, the Little Grace has been on the cocktail list, where Nick says it will "probably stay forever." For a perfect serve, be sure to use good apple liqueur, not the fluorescent green stuff.

GLASSWARE: Coupe glass

GARNISH: Cinnamon sugar

- 1 oz. | 30 ml Żubrówka Bison Grass Vodka
- 1 oz. | 30 ml G.E. Massenez Green Apple Liqueur
- ⅔ oz. | 20 ml cloudy apple juice
- ⅔ oz. | 20 ml fresh lemon juice
- ½ oz. | 15 ml G.E. Massenez Elderflower Liqueur
- ½ oz. | 15 ml spiced simple syrup
- Dash egg white

1. Combine all of the ingredients in a Boston shaker.
2. Top with ice and shake.
3. Double-strain the cocktail into a champagne saucer.
4. Garnish with a very light dusting of cinnamon sugar.

FARMER'S MARKET

BURROW BAR
BASEMENT/96 CLARENCE ST, SYDNEY

Burrow Bar co-owner Chau Tran says owning a small bar in YCK Laneways is like living in the neighborhood of the best bars in Australia and your best pals. The Farmer's Market encapsulates the pleasures of meandering through a local market, using the best ingredients from local producers and creating a seasonal drink, with notes of coconut, cognac, strawberries, and sencha tea that is then clarified—clear and crisp, sparkling in the glass. This is a labor of love: the clarification takes a minimum of 12 hours, but it's worth every minute. Makes multiple servings.

GLASSWARE: Rocks glass
GARNISH: Fresh chamomile flower or marigold

- 6¾ oz. | 200 ml Never Never Distilling Co. Juniper Freak Gin
- 2⅔ oz. | 80 ml chamomile tea
- 2⅔ oz. | 80 grams Greek yogurt
- 1 oz. | 30 ml honey syrup
- 1 teaspoon | 5 ml Aperol, to top

1. In a mixing glass, combine all of the ingredients, except for the Aperol. This mixture should be left to sit for 12 hours at room temperature.

2. Strain the cocktail through a coffee filter.

3. Pour 3 oz. (90 ml) over a big, clear ice cube into a rocks glass.

4. Garnish with fresh flowers and top with Aperol.

MANGO WEISSY MARTINI

CASH ONLY DINER
1 BARRACK ST, SYDNEY

C ash Only Diner specializes in food from Hue and Da Nang and
this unique championing of the beautiful regionality of Vietnamese cuisine has made it a destination for foodies. The drinks are made
by Chau Tran, who is a Global Gin Mare champion. The Mango
Weissy Martini is a playful riff on an Australian classic ice-cream, the
Mango Weiss bar.

Green mango–infused vermouth and a nutty gin that has been coconut fat–washed make this Martini luscious. Notes of green apple
and mango very gently sing alongside the coconut notes. It pairs perfectly with the Hue cuisine.

GLASSWARE: Rocks glass

- 17 oz. | 500 ml Lady Triêu Gin
- 1¾ oz. | 50 grams coconut oil
- 17 oz. | 500 ml Noilly Prat Original Dry Vermouth
- 5 oz. | 140 grams Thai green mango

1. The ratio of gin to vermouth is 4:3—4 parts coconut gin and 3 parts mango vermouth. Overnight preparation is required for both.

2. Vacuum-pack the gin and coconut oil and leave the mixture in a warm spot for 3 hours.

3. Cut the skin and flesh of a Thai green mango into ⅖ in. (1 cm) slices.

4. Freeze the oil and gin overnight. Steep the mango slices in the vermouth overnight in the refrigerator.

5. Strain and bottle the fat-washed gin. Strain the vermouth.

6. Mix the mango-infused vermouth and the coconut fat–washed gin together and serve in a rocks glass over ice.

FUEGO DE ESTEBAN

Visitors to Esteban, a split-level New York–style underground venue, are met with a giant display of spirits. "We strive to have the most extensive collection of agave spirits in Australia, with well-trained bartenders ready to give you a journey of our fresh and vibrant cocktails, " says co-owner and executive bar manager Mark Crawford.

With mezcal speeding up the ranks of go-to spirits for Sydney drinkers, the Fuego de Esteban was created to match the venue. This fun twist on the Martinez is dark and moody with a smoky, fiery kick to it.

GLASSWARE: Rocks glass

GARNISH: Chile pepper and 2 olives on a skewer

- ⅚ oz. | 25 ml mezcal gin
- ⅔ oz. | 20 ml Dolin Rouge Vermouth
- ½ oz. | 15 ml Luxardo Maraschino Originale
- 1 teaspoon | 5 ml agave nectar
- Dash habanero bitters

1. In a mixing glass, stir all of the ingredients over ice.

2. When mixed, strain the cocktail into a rocks glass filled with ice.

3. Garnish with a skewer of 2 chile pepper slices and 2 olives.

JONOTHAN CARR, THE CHARLES GRAND BRASSERIE & BAR AND TIVA

An art deco building in the center of Sydney's CBD is home to the elegant The Charles Grand Brasserie & Bar and Tiva basement lounge. Director of bars Jonothan Carr aims to provide table service with a dash of understated theater at both venues. An Old Fashioned with single malt whiskey and cognac, for example, is served table-side in a three-piece, bottle-shaped decanter. In front of guests, Jonothan unstacks the iced glassware then pours the carefully made Old Fashioned from the decanter. The Tequila Martini with rose vermouth is shaken and poured table-side, while the Espresso Martini is created in an elaborate French press.

Martinis are consistently among the bars' top-selling drinks. They are so popular that Jonothan's next cocktail menu will have a whole section dedicated to them.

He believes that as people choose to drink less but better, the Martini makes a wonderful choice. Jonothan has also found guests are more knowledgeable about spirits than ever, they know what their favorite vodka or gin is and they want to enjoy it in a beverage that lets it shine.

THE CHARLES MARTINI

THE CHARLES BAR
66 KING ST, SYDNEY

The Charles Martini arrives at the table incredibly cold and with several garnish options for the guests to make it their own—Jonothan Carr believes that, by giving guests the chance to choose when they zest the drink or add olives or pickled onions, the bar encourages them to create their own rituals surrounding Martinis. Carr has imported Japanese chilled sake decanters, which allow him and his bartenders to fill a section with ice to keep Martinis cold on their way to customers. The Charles Bar keeps its Martini glasses and spirits in the bar's freezer at -19°C (-2°F). A great Martini is the sum of its parts, he says: an amazing vodka or gin deserves a quality vermouth and perfect dilution. A dash of orange bitters is a nice touch.

GLASSWARE: Martini glass
GARNISH: Lemon coin, green olive, pickled onion, dropper
of onion brine

- 2⅓ oz. | 65 ml Absolut Elyx or Beefeater Gin
- ⅓ oz. | 10 ml Regal Rogue Lively White Vermouth
- ⅓ oz. | 10 ml filtered water
- 1 teaspoon | 5 ml Lillet Blanc
- 1/32 oz. | 1 ml orange bitters

1. Combine all of the ingredients and store in a freezer at -2°F (-19°C).

2. Ensure the martini glass is super frozen before serving the cocktail.

3. Garnish with a lemon coin, green olive, pickled onion, and a dropper of onion brine (start with 3 drops and go from there).

BENEATH THE SHEETS

TIVA LOUNGE
68 KING ST, SYDNEY

Director of bars Jonothan Carr says this take on a Cosmopolitan is fresh and vibrant, like Sydney, a city that is constantly changing while, underneath, it remains the city Sydneysiders know and love. "We pre-batch the cocktail and add dilution so all the elements have time to combine together. This also means we can whip up the beverage swiftly for our guests," Jonothan says, adding, "A flamed orange disk gives a touch of theater and adds aroma to the serve."

GLASSWARE: Rocks glass

GARNISH: Flamed orange disk

- 1 oz. | 30 ml Citrus Peel–Infused Blanco Tequila (see recipe)
- ⅚ oz. | 25 ml cranberry juice
- ⅔ oz. | 20 ml honey-and-cinnamon cordial
- ½ oz. | 15 ml dry orange liqueur
- ⅓ oz. | 10 ml filtered water

1. Combine all of the ingredients together and allow the mixture to rest in the refrigerator for 2 days.

2. When it's time to serve, pour the cocktail over quality ice in a large rocks glass and stir.

3. Garnish with a flamed orange disk.

CITRUS PEEL–INFUSED BLANCO TEQUILA: Peel 2 limes, 1 lemon, and 1 pink grapefruit. Place the peels in a sealable jar, then pour in a bottle of quality blanco tequila, seal the jar, and leave it to steep at room temperature for 24 hours. Strain out the peels. You can use the citrus fruit for other cocktails while you wait for the infusion to complete.

EXTRA! EXTRA!

Owner Lara Dignam says the Extra! Extra! is very Sydney, in that it's a take on fads, or the constant lure of the newest, most Insta-worthy things to do and places to be seen. The cocktail is created with a house-made blue curaçao syrup (featuring a secret, natural blue ingredient), which pays homage to the stunning blues of the Harbour City. The perfect serve, says Lara, is the one that makes your customer the happiest. It could be different every time. Good quality ice is a must, though.

GLASSWARE: Coupette or small martini glass
GARNISH: Scented smoke bubble (optional) or lemon zest

- 1 oz. | 30 ml vodka
- ½ oz. | 15 ml Italicus Rosolio di Bergamotto
- 1 oz. | 30 ml fresh lemon juice
- ½ oz. | 15 ml Blue Curaçao Syrup (see recipe)

1. Add all of the ingredients to a cocktail shaker and fill the shaker with the best ice possible.

2. Shake hard until the mixture is very cold.

3. Double-strain the cocktail into a coupette or small martini glass.

4. Garnish with a scented smoke bubble or, if you're not that fancy, a lovely bit of lemon zest will do.

BLUE CURAÇAO SYRUP: Experiment with natural ingredients (sugar, orange peel, secret herbs and spices) to achieve the color you are after. Blueberries and blue spirulina powder are a good place to begin. Or use store-bought syrup (both Torani and Monin make it).

AFRICOLA

PS40 owner and bartender Michael Chiem says it's his culinary approach to drinks that helps attract many returning guests. The Africola has taken on a life of its own, with guests often visiting the bar so their friends can try the cocktail. It has contrasting temperatures of 158°F (70°C) and 14°F (-10°C) at the same time. "We also make a native wattleseed cola that goes with it and a warm coconut foam that floats above," he says.

GLASSWARE: Pint glass

- 2⅔ oz. | 80 ml Wattle Cola
- 1 oz. | 30 ml Mr Black Cold Brew Coffee Liqueur, frozen
- 2 oz. | 60 ml Warm Coconut Foam (see recipe)

1. Add the cola to a large pint glass.

2. Add the frozen liqueur. This reduces any foam that may occur.

3. Charge off the warm coconut foam into a warm vessel and then slowly layer the foam on top.

WARM COCONUT FOAM:
In a 17 oz. (500 ml) siphon, add
4 ¼ oz. (120 grams) granulated
sugar, 13 ½ oz. (400 ml) coconut cream, 13 ½ oz. (400 ml)
coconut milk, and 7 oz.
(207 ml) pure cream. Bring this
up to temperature on a 158°F
(70°C) sous vide and let it sit
for 5 minutes. Charge the
siphon with 2 bulbs, shaking
vigorously in between. This
makes 1 liter (34 oz.).

SIMON ROSE-HOPKINS, JOLENE'S

Simon Rose-Hopkins is passionate about two things: whiskey and the bright lights and bold nightlife of Nashville. He has combined those two loves at Jolene's, where the atmosphere is dark, moody, and loud, but the drinking experience is designed to inform and educate.

Jolene's unites a global whiskey collection that spans top-shelf American classics as well as Scottish, Japanese, and new Australian blends with an American diner–style menu. Simon is the former licensee of Surly's American BBQ, bar manager of NOLA Smokehouse & Bar, and has also been a whiskey brand ambassador for Bacardi.

"The bar is my way of paying homage to some of the best nights of my life and bringing that genuine Southern hospitality to York Street," he says.

The Southern hospitality continues with booths being named after country singers: Chris Stapleton, Kenny Rogers, Johnny Cash, Taylor Swift (for those more mainstream country lovers), and, for the twelve-seater VIP booth, Dolly Parton. With live music, the venue quickly turns into a party on Thursday, Friday, and Saturday nights. The lineup supports local country and rock bands, with the bar deliberately placed on the opposite end of the venue to the stage so guests can interact with the bar team while the music is playing.

TENNESSEE TRUCK STOP

JOLENE'S
73 YORK ST, SYDNEY

Simon Rose-Hopkins' Tennessee Truck Stop cocktail is a homage to his two favorite cities: Sydney and Nashville. According to Simon, there is nothing more "Sydney" than getting a piece of toasted banana bread with your morning coffee, something he has not found anywhere else on his travels. "My cocktail tastes like a toasted banana bread with a vanilla latte," he says. "If you're making this at home, use purified water for your ice—a lot of home cocktail makers neglect the ice that they use in their drinks."

GLASSWARE: Old-fashioned glass

GARNISH: Dehydrated banana chip, orange rind

- 1½ oz. | 45 ml Jack Daniel's Old No. 7 Tennessee Whiskey
- ⅓ oz. | 10 ml Tempus Fugit Crème de Banane
- 1 teaspoon | 5 ml vanilla syrup
- 4 dashes Fee Brothers Black Walnut Bitters

1. Chill an old-fashioned glass. Add all of the ingredients to a mixing glass and stir with a spoon.

2. Place a whiskey ice block in the chilled old-fashioned glass. Pour the cocktail over the ice.

3. Garnish with a dehydrated banana chip and, after twisting it over the drink to express its oils, an orange rind.

BARBER SHOP GIMLET

THE BARBER SHOP
89 YORK ST, SYDNEY

Gin is Sydney's favorite spirit, and The Barber Shop has a collection of more than 700 kinds of gin. The Barber Shop Gimlet pairs native ingredients with Asian flavors and the result is a combination that is truly different. There is nowhere to hide in a drink with so few ingredients, and the access to a solid base liquid and fresh produce ensures success.

GLASSWARE: Rocks glass
GARNISH: Kaffir lime leaf

- 1½ oz. | 45 ml Hickson Rd. London Dry Gin
- 1 oz. | 30 ml finger lime cordial
- 1 teaspoon | 5 ml coriander tincture

1. Stir all of the ingredients briskly together in a mixing glass with ice blocks until the mixture is very chilled but not overdiluted.

2. Strain the cocktail into a rocks glass over the biggest clear ice cube that fits the glass snugly.

3. Bruise a kaffir lime leaf gently to release its aroma and place it on top of the clear ice.

ESPRESSO MARTINI

SAMMY JUNIOR
66 KING ST, SYDNEY

Bridging the worlds of coffee and cocktails, Sammy Junior is a suave hot spot offering bespoke coffee varieties, classic breakfast bites, and sandwiches and salads by day. As the sun sets, the venue transforms into a midcity cocktail destination. Founded by Vince Lombardo, Stefano Catino, and Martin Hudak, this is the sister venue to one of the city's most awarded cocktail bars, Maybe Sammy, and offers the same level of hospitality and attention to detail. Venue manager Claudio Bedini advises that both the coffee liqueur and rum should be well chilled, and the textures and flavors will be enhanced by aerating the cocktail in a frappe machine rather than shaking.

GLASSWARE: Martini glass

GARNISH: Cracked cocoa nibs, rock salt

- 1⅓ oz. | 40 ml Mr Black Cold Brew Coffee Liqueur
- ⅔ oz. | 20 ml Bacardí Reserva Ocho
- 1 oz. | 30 ml fresh-brewed espresso
- 2⅔ oz. | 80 ml coconut water, cold

1. Combine all of the ingredients and whip them together in a frappe machine to aerate.

2. Pour the cocktail into a martini glass and garnish with cracked cocoa nibs and rock salt.

The Boathouse at Balmoral

NORTH

DAWN

PEACHES & CREAM

HOKEY SMOKEY

PETERMEN NEGRONI

BEE STILL

GREEN MOUSTACHE

NATIVE GINGER

RHUBARB MARG

THE CUMBERLAND

LAVENDER BAY

SOCAL MARGARITA

OYSTER SHELL MARTINI

FRAGOLA FIZZ

MEZCAL PALOMA

Travel north of the iconic Sydney Harbour Bridge to discover a burgeoning bar scene that offers everything from bustling after-work venues in the North Sydney business district to bars that feel a thousand miles from the city. Catch a ferry from Circular Quay in Sydney's CBD to Manly to explore venues such as The Cumberland, Poetica, and Banco, which are pushing the envelope on what is expected from beachside bars and elevating the overall offerings in the process.

From Manly, a string of surf beaches extends for 18½ miles (30 km) to Palm Beach, the setting for one of Australia's most globally famed TV melodramas, *Home & Away.*

DAWN

Light-filled Poetica opens out onto a covered terrace overlooking the bustling street below, and prides itself on its refined but relaxed atmosphere. The cocktail list features thoughtful uses of Australian ingredients, and the back bar focuses on great Australian spirits. Former The Barber Shop and Rockpool Bar & Grill Perth alumnus Kieran Lee heads up the bar experience as bar manager. "Dawn is made using a gin distilled just across the Sydney Harbour Bridge—Hickson House Distilling Co.," he explains. "The pickle brine uses the same botanicals that go into the gin to brighten the cocktail, which makes for a great local take on a Bloody Mary."

GLASSWARE: Highball glass

GARNISH: Lemon slice and olive on a skewer

- 1½ oz. | 45 ml Hickson Rd. Seven Spice Gin
- 1½ oz. | 45 ml tomato juice
- ⅔ oz. | 20 ml fresh lemon juice
- ½ oz. | 15 ml apera or dry sherry
- ½ oz. | 15 ml pickle brine
- ⅓ oz. | 10 ml fermented chile peppers

1. Add all of the ingredients to a mixing glass with ice.

2. Stir until the outside of the shaker feels very cold.

3. Strain the cocktail into a highball glass and garnish with a lemon slice and olive skewered together.

KURTIS BOSLEY, BANCO MANLY, CORRETTO

Award-winning bartender and social media cocktail influencer Kurtis Bosley (@cocktailsbykurtis) owns and operates two bars on Sydney's Northern Beaches: Banco and Corretto. Banco is hidden away in the back streets of Manly and has a Manhattan vibe. It aims to delight guests who enjoy escapism and discovery. Further north in Dee Why is Corretto, which has spectacular ocean views that draw locals and visitors in equal measure.

"If somebody doesn't leave my bar happier than when they arrived, I haven't done my job," says Kurtis of his philosophy.

While his cocktail menus are technique driven, Kurtis focuses on "taking the ego out of drink menu listings" and highlighting key flavors that will delight his guests by taking them on a journey of cocktail exploration. The results, as Kurtis puts it, are "simple deliciousness."

PEACHES & CREAM

BANCO MANLY
7B WHISTLER ST, MANLY

A recent focus for Kurtis has been on elevating the appreciation of whiskey in cocktails. He has a particular affinity with Glenmorangie, which he describes as being the most forward-thinking, creative, and inclusive whiskey on the market today, the "Willy Wonka of the whisky world."

He says the hint of smoke found in the whiskey adds a new layer of flavor to the cocktail-and-food pairings he champions at Banco. "In a stirred-down Old Fashioned, balanced Sour, or sparkling Highball, whisky has all the layers and complexity you could need," he explains.

GLASSWARE: Highball glass

GARNISH: Citrus Foam (see recipe)

- 1⅓ oz. | 40 ml X by Glenmorangie
- ⅔ oz. | 20 ml verjus
- ⅓ oz. | 10 ml peach wine
- ½ oz. | 15 ml silver needle white tea
- ⅓ oz. | 10 ml Mancino Secco Vermouth

1. Add all of the ingredients to a shaker and add ice.

2. Shake hard, then single-strain the cocktail into a highball glass.

3. Garnish with citrus foam.

CITRUS FOAM: Add 4 oz. (120 ml) water, 2 egg whites, and 1⅓ oz. (40 ml) fresh lemon juice to a soda siphon. Charge with 2 chargers.

HOKEY SMOKEY

CORRETTO
1/24 THE STRAND, DEE WHY

A bar by the beach is quintessentially Sydney and Kurtis Bosley says a long drink that is carbonated and fun is the most popular order for both locals and visitors. Overlooking the ocean at Dee Why, Corretto attracts plenty of walk-in guests and serves up drinks that sound mouth-watering and taste even better. The secret to a perfect cocktail, he says, is to control the dilution and always use quality ice.

GLASSWARE: Collins glass

GARNISH: Raspberry leather (optional)

- 1 oz. | 30 ml Ardbeg Five Years Old

- ⅚ oz. | 25 ml Spiced Raspberry and Tonka Syrup (see recipe)

- ½ oz. | 15 ml apricot brandy

- ⅔ oz. | 20 ml fresh lemon juice

- 2 dashes whiskey barrel–aged bitters

- Soda water, to top

1. Add all of the ingredients, except the soda water, to a cocktail shaker.

2. Add ice and shake the drink hard.

3. Double-strain the cocktail into a collins glass and top with soda water.

4. Garnish with raspberry leather if you like.

SPICED RASPBERRY AND TONKA SYRUP: Add 21 oz. (600 grams) superfine (caster) sugar, 18 oz. (500 grams) frozen raspberries, 18 oz. (500 ml) water, 3 ½ oz. (100 ml) cranberry juice, 2 cloves, 1 cinnamon stick, 1 vanilla pod, and ⁷⁄₁₀ oz. (2 grams) citric acid to a medium saucepan and bring the mixture to a boil. Grate 4 tonka beans into the saucepan and boil for 30 minutes. Lower the heat to a simmer and cook for 1 hour. Remove the pan from heat and add salt, to taste, and stir. Let the syrup sit for 2 hours before straining it.

PETERMEN NEGRONI

PETERMEN
66 CHANDOS ST, ST LEONARDS

Owner Josh Niland sought the assistance of his friend and award-winning bartender Evan Stroeve to build the cocktail list at Petermen in St Leonards. The beauty of the Petermen Negroni is that you can set it and forget it at home when entertaining. Batch everything together before your guests arrive and store it in the freezer to get it cold. When you're ready, pour it directly over ice and forget about any messy cleanup.

GLASSWARE: Rocks glass
GARNISH: Citrus peel

- 6¾ oz. | 200 ml yuzushu
- 6¾ oz. | 200 ml Campari
- 5 oz. | 150 ml Punt e Mes
- 20 drops kombu bitters

- ¾ oz. | 200 ml Archie Rose Signature Dry Gin
- 4¼ oz. | 125 ml water
- 4¼ oz. | 125 ml coconut water

1. Add all of the ingredients to a bottle or Tupperware container.

2. Put the ingredients in the freezer for 1 or 2 hours.

3. To serve, pour a generous helping of the mixture over good quality ice in a rocks glass.

4. Garnish with a twist of your favorite citrus peel.

BEE STILL

ALMA
47 OLD BARRENJOEY RD, AVALON BEACH

When bartender Austin Andrews-Little turns his mind to a Sydney cocktail, he thinks of the natural ingredients of the land to showcase the beauty of Australia's native flora and fauna. With some of the most spectacular honey in the world being made in local Avalon apiaries, and rosemary and elderflower growing wildly around every corner of Sydney, he says the Bee Still cocktail's flavors best embody what his city has to offer.

GLASSWARE: Lowball glass

GARNISH: Lightly smoked rosemary sprig

- ⅓ oz. | 10 ml elderflower liqueur
- ⅓ oz. | 10 ml Rosemary Syrup (see recipe)
- ⅓ oz. | 10 ml honey water (2:1)
- ⅔ oz. | 20 ml rye whiskey
- ⅔ oz. | 20 ml fresh lemon juice
- ½ oz. | 15 ml mezcal
- ½ oz. | 15 ml aquafaba

1. Combine all of the ingredients in a cocktail shaker over ice and shake until the outside of the tin is frosted.

2. Strain out the ice and shake again to create foam.

3. Fine-strain the drink over ice into a lowball glass and garnish with a lightly smoked rosemary sprig.

ROSEMARY SYRUP: Heat 1 cup (240 ml) water and 1 cup (240 ml) granulated sugar in a pot and stir until the sugar has fully dissolved. Transfer the syrup into a bottle and add 4 sprigs of fresh rosemary to steep overnight. The next day, fine-strain out the rosemary and try your homemade rosemary syrup.

GREEN MOUSTACHE

GREEN MOUSTACHE
ROOFTOP, LEVEL 10/100 MILLER ST, NORTH SYDNEY

Rooftop bar Green Moustache is hidden in North Sydney's business district. Up among the trees, the venue has become popular with office workers looking to relax after their workday. The eponymous Green Moustache cocktail was designed with the bar's green leafy outlook in mind and is the most popular drink on the menu.

GLASSWARE: Wineglass

GARNISH: Cucumber slice

- Cucumber, to taste
- 1 oz. | 30 ml Roku Gin
- 1 oz. | 30 ml G.E. Massenez Green Apple Liqueur
- 1 oz. | 30 ml fresh lime juice
- 1 oz. | 20 ml green apple syrup
- Dash Sprite

1. In the bottom of a cocktail shaker, muddle the cucumber.

2. Add all of the remaining ingredients, except for the Sprite, and shake with ice.

3. Double-strain the cocktail into a wineglass.

4. Add a scoop of ice and a dash of Sprite.

5. Garnish with a large slice of cucumber.

NATIVE GINGER

BAR ELVINA
50 OLD BARRENJOEY RD, AVALON BEACH

Boasting a cult following with locals, Bar Elvina swells in the warmer months with visitors drawn to Sydney's Northern Beaches. The Native Ginger, a twist on a Margarita, was created to satisfy the Sydney crowd's love of anything tequila. It uses Amaro Montenegro and native rainforest ginger, which gives a spicy, sour flavor similar to that of common ginger, but with a little more acidity. The flavors are amped up with house-made ginger syrup.

GLASSWARE: Lowball glass

GARNISH: Ginger leaf

- 1½ oz. | 45 ml Tromba Blanco Tequila
- 1 oz. | 30 ml fresh lemon juice
- 1 oz. | 30 ml ginger syrup
- ⅔ oz. | 20 ml Amaro Montenegro
- Rosemary-infused honey, to taste

1. Stir all of the ingredients together in a mixing glass.

2. Serve over block ice in a lowball glass, garnished with a fresh ginger leaf.

RHUBARB MARG

LITTLE PEARL BAR
8/13 SOUTH STEYNE, MANLY

Little Pearl Bar is a gem hidden away from the hustle and bustle of the Corso, with uninterrupted views of the beach. Venue manager Simone Traves-Taylor says the Rhubarb Marg is just like Sydney: it's fun, a little spicy, and it will leave a lingering sensation on your lips. She notes that quality ingredients and balance are important to ensure the perfect serve. Habanero peppers are dry-roasted in a frying pan before the drink's signature syrup is made. Staff carefully check the syrup to ensure the spice of the habaneros comes through the rhubarb without overwhelming the taste buds.

GLASSWARE: Coupe glass

- 1½ oz. | 45 ml tequila
- 1 oz. | 30 ml Rhubarb and Habanero Pepper Syrup (see recipe)
- 1 oz. | 30 ml fresh lime juice
- ½ oz. | 15 ml sake
- ½ oz. | 15 ml passion fruit puree
- Salt, for the rim
- Chile pepper flakes, for the rim

1. Combine all of the ingredients, except the salt and chile pepper flakes, in a cocktail shaker with ice.

2. Hard-shake, then double-strain the cocktail into a coupe glass rimmed with salt and chile pepper flakes.

RHUBARB AND HABANERO PEPPER SYRUP: In a medium saucepan over high heat, add 4 cups water, 2 cups chopped rhubarb, 2 cups sugar, and 1 chopped habanero, with seeds and bring the mixture to a boil. Lower the heat and simmer for 20 minutes. Allow the syrup to cool then strain it through a fine-mesh sieve. It will keep in the refrigerator for 1 month.

THE CUMBERLAND

THE CUMBERLAND
17-19 CENTRAL AVE, MANLY

The Cumberland is an underground speakeasy with a Spanish twist. Located in the Parish of Manly Cove in the County of Cumberland, its name is a nod to the history of the area. Concealed behind a fridge door within a small, bodega-style deli, the sophisticated basement bar's décor speaks to the era of Prohibition, with ornate and vintage furnishings, including marble benchtops, hand-carved sandstone blocks, reclaimed wood, antique brass and copper accents, and a handmade leather banquette seat that wraps the walls of the intimate venue. General manager Pete Ehemann wanted to create a single malt Scotch cocktail to introduce guests to whiskey cocktails. The result is Cumberland's eponymous cocktail, which is sweet and smoky and very approachable.

GLASSWARE: Coupette glass
GARNISH: Cherry wood smoke, 2 or 3 griottes on a skewer

- 1½ oz. | 45 ml The Glenlivet Caribbean Reserve
- 1 oz. | 30 ml cherry puree
- ⅓ oz. | 10 ml Pedro Ximénez
- ⅓ oz. | 10 ml honey water

1. Chill a coupette glass. Combine all of the ingredients in a cocktail shaker with ice and shake.

2. Fine-strain the cocktail into the chilled coupette.

3. Using a cloche, garnish with cherry wood smoke, then add 2 or 3 skewered griottes (brandied sour cherries).

LAVENDER BAY

LOULOU
61 LAVENDER ST, MILSONS POINT

Loulou is set in the gorgeous harborside enclave of Lavender Bay and prides itself on having a neighborhood feel. Bar director Jonothan Carr says the Lavender Bay takes cues from the local environment, including the lavender that grows locally and the waterside location.

GLASSWARE: Coupette glass
GARNISH: Sprig of dried lavender

- 1⅕ oz. | 35 ml vodka
- 1 oz. | 30 ml fresh pineapple juice
- ½ oz. | 15 ml lavender syrup
- ⅓ oz| 10 ml crème de violette
- ⅓ oz. | 10 ml fresh lemon juice
- 1 egg white (or aquafaba)

1. Chill a coupette glass. Combine all of the ingredients together in a cocktail shaker and dry-shake.

2. Add ice and shake until frothy. This extra shake to emulsify the liquids will ensure a nice frothy cocktail.

3. Strain the cocktail into the chilled coupette and garnish with a sprig of dried lavender.

SOCAL MARGARITA

SOCAL
I YOUNG ST, NEUTRAL BAY

Sydney is known for its beachy vibes, and SoCal bar manager Tristan Fisher says it feels like summer all year round at his venue, which has a rooftop terrace that is the perfect spot to enjoy the sunshine. SoCal set out to make a cocktail that tastes like the beach with its signature Margarita. Refreshing citrus balances the sweet tequila and a salt rim to ensure it feels like you are drinking a vacation in a glass.

GLASSWARE: Margarita glass

- 1½ oz. | 45 ml blanco tequila
- 1 oz. | 30 ml fresh lime juice
- ½ oz. | 15 ml orange curaçao
- ⅓ oz. | 10 ml simple syrup
- Salt, for the rim

1. Combine all of the ingredients in a cocktail shaker and shake.

2. Serve the cocktail in a margarita glass with a half salt rim.

OYSTER SHELL MARTINI

RANDY'S
50 OLD BARRENJOEY RD, AVALON BEACH

I t's a hop, skip, and a jump to the ocean from Randy's at Avalon Beach, and the saline notes of Never Never Oyster Shell Gin in the bar's signature Martini pair perfectly with the oyster brine, resulting in aquatic euphoria for imbibers. The cocktail is offered in a 8 ½ oz. (250 ml) carafe—owner Andrew Emerson's philosophy, when it comes to Martinis, is the bigger the better.

GLASSWARE: Martini glass
GARNISH: Lemon peel twist, freshly shucked oyster

- 2 oz. | 60 ml Never Never Oyster Shell Gin
- ⅓ oz | 10 ml Dolin Dry Vermouth

1. Chill a martini glass. Stir the gin, vermouth, and a little ice together in a mixing glass.

2. Strain the cocktail into the chilled martini glass.

3. Serve with a twist of lemon peel and a freshly shucked oyster (Randy's serves NSW South Coast oysters).

FRAGOLA FIZZ

RAFI
99 MOUNT ST, NORTH SYDNEY

There is nothing modest about the Fragola Fizz. Created for Sydney, it's citrusy, playful, slightly bitter, and slightly sweet. Adding carbonation to the drink makes it extra lively, which matches its vibrant red appearance. Bar manager Cameron Freno recommends serving the Fragola Fizz very cold at around 35.6°F (2°C). "This will help the overall carbonation and reduce dilution, creating better consistency," he says.

GLASSWARE: Rocks glass
GARNISH: Spiced Aperol Strawberry Fruit Leather (see recipe)

- ⅔ oz. | 20 ml Aperol infused with strawberries and Szechuan peppercorns
- ⅔ oz. | 20 ml vodka
- ⅔ oz. | 20 ml agave syrup
- ⅔ oz. | 20 ml water
- ½ oz. | 15 ml yuzu sake
- ⅖ oz. | 12.5 ml fresh lemon juice
- ⅖ oz. | 12.5 ml fresh lime juice
- Citrus Dust (see recipe), for the rim

1. Combine all of the ingredients, except the citrus dust, in a mixing glass.

2. Wet the rim of a rocks glass then dip the glass rim in the citrus dust.

3. Pour the cocktail into the rocks glass and top with ice.

4. Garnish with fruit leather.

SPICED APEROL STRAWBERRY FRUIT LEATHER: Using the strawberries and Szechuan peppercorns from the Aperol infusion, blend them together with a mixture of lemon juice and sugar, to taste. Then dehydrate these sheets for 8 hours on low temperature, in an oven or food dehydrator, until they set as fruit leather.

CITRUS DUST: Either using a dehydrator or an oven set to its lowest temperature, dehydrate lemon, lime, orange, and/or grapefruit slices to your liking. Combine the dried fruits in a blender and blend until the mixture reaches a powder.

MEZCAL PALOMA

THE BOATHOUSE
2 THE ESPLANADE, MOSMAN

I f you were tasked with building a dream beach from scratch, the finished product would be Balmoral Beach, the jewel in the crown of Sydney Harbour's beaches—the wide strip of sand and calm water are perfect for swimming and water sports. The Boathouse's Mezcal Paloma is the go-to cocktail that stays on the menu year round. Pretty in pink, it is a refreshing yet smoky choice, ideal for sipping while the sun sets over the water.

GLASSWARE: Double old-fashioned glass

GARNISH: Ruby red grapefruit wedge

- Sea salt flakes, for the rim
- Tajín, for the rim
- 1 oz. | 30 ml grapefruit syrup
- 1 oz. | 30 ml fresh lime juice

- ⅔ oz. | 20 ml tequila
- ⅔ oz. | 20 ml triple sec
- ⅔ oz. | 20 ml mezcal

1. Wet the rim of a double old-fashioned glass then dip the glass rim in a mixture of sea salt flakes and Tajín.

2. Pour all of the remaining ingredients into a cocktail shaker.

3. Add ice and shake for 5 seconds.

4. Strain the cocktail into the glass.

5. Top with ice cubes and garnish with a wedge of ruby red grapefruit.

Bondi Beach from the Promenade

EAST

NO. 147

WARATAH SPRITZ

WATERMELON DAIQUIRI

ARMY & NAVY

THE CHAPALA CANTARITO

SANCHEZ PALOMA

LOTTIE DENO

PORNSTAR MARTINI

PISCO SOUR

SALTED CARAMEL RUM

OLD FASHIONED

YULEFEST RECORDS

COCO BONGO

JULEP RE-FASHIONED

ELECTRIC MARGARITA

SHIRAZ ME NOT

CAMPARI FRAISE

WATERMELON SUGAR

SANDPRINT

PLEASE & THANK YOU

FORRY'S BLOODY MARY

CARLOTTA

Sydney's eastern suburbs stretch from the grit and glitter of inner-city Darlinghurst, home of the Sydney Gay and Lesbian Mardi Gras, to the dazzling aquamarine shores of the Pacific Ocean. It's there you will find one of the world's most famous stretches of sand, Bondi Beach. At its center is the heritage-listed Bondi Pavilion, which was built in the Georgian revival and Mediterranean styles in 1929 and restored in 2022.

Sydney East is also home to the infamous red-light district, Kings Cross—or "The Cross" as locals fondly refer to it—which was the birthplace of Sydney's modern bar scene and remains a vibrant nightlife hub.

Some of Sydney's most acclaimed bars are nestled on the streets between the city and the sea, clustered in the character-filled suburbs of Paddington and Darlinghurst.

The East's glamorous beaches can be reached in less than twenty minutes from the CBD and the views from the bars and restaurants that overlook on their shores are stunning.

You'll find everything from casual hole-in-the-wall establishments to high-end bars and heritage pubs serving innovative cocktail creations that reflect Sydneysiders' obsession with sand and sea.

MATTY OPAI, ICEBERGS BAR

Perched on the cliffs overlooking historic Bondi Baths and the sparkling sand of Bondi Beach is Icebergs Bar, where bar director Matty Opai mixes cocktails while drinking in one of the most spectacular views in Australia. Opai says people come from all over the world not just to see Icebergs, but, perhaps more importantly, to be seen at Icebergs.

His regulars return because he treats them like family, with his staff priding themselves on remembering people's names, their favorite drinks, and where they work. As you sit at Icebergs, looking out over the world-famous beach, time seems to slow down, and all the worries in life slowly slip to the back of your mind.

Opai's brief with the cocktail list at Icebergs is Italian beachside drinking. His service style is polished, low-key, and elegant, ensuring the iconic view is at the forefront of people's attention.

ICEBERGS
I NOTTS AVE, BONDI BEACH

While there has been a resurgence of spirit-forward cocktails such as the Negroni and Old Fashioned, Matty Opai says many Sydneysiders still love fruity, tiki-inspired drinks. The No. 147 has been a mainstay on the Icebergs drinks list for the past ten years and remains its number one bestseller. The idea behind it was to create a Piña-Colada-esque cocktail, sans the cream . . . which Opai jokes is "very Bondi!" A good, hard shake is necessary for this drink to truly shine. According to him, if you only give it the "old lazy one-two, you will get an overly viscous acid bomb that will call for a Gaviscon soon after." A lengthier, solid shake gives the drink the vibrancy it deserves, aerating the cocktail and resulting in a foamy consistency that should be enjoyed immediately, before the ingredients settle and split.

GLASSWARE: Wineglass

GARNISH: Lime wedge

- 1⅓ oz. | 40 ml Belvedere Vodka
- 1⅓ oz. | 40 ml pineapple juice
- ⅔ oz. | 20 ml Joseph Cartron Coconut Liqueur

- ½ oz. | 15 ml falernum
- ½ oz. | 15 ml fresh lime juice
- ½ oz. | 15 ml passion fruit puree
- Dash old-fashioned bitters

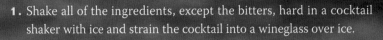

1. Shake all of the ingredients, except the bitters, hard in a cocktail shaker with ice and strain the cocktail into a wineglass over ice.

2. Add a dash of bitters and garnish the drink with a lime wedge to serve.

EVAN STROEVE, THE WARATAH

Award-winning bartender Evan Stroeve recently celebrated opening his first bar, The Waratah, in inner-city Darlinghurst. The bar is named after the crimson waratah, the state flower of NSW (New South Wales), which is as striking as it is iconic. The bloom represents the bar's celebration of modern Australia and its magnificent diversity. Digging deep into seasonal ingredients and their producers, The Waratah's farm-to-glass model places produce at the heart of the experience.

Stroeve has a purpose to his work, aiming to reconnect people to the things they consume and showcase Australia's biological diversity and flavor potential. He loves to see the look on customers' faces when they try something "new and awesome."

"When they're having fun and laughing, I cherish being able to be a part of that. I love the frenetic energy of a busy night," he says.

According to Stroeve, the secret to ensuring customers feel welcome in a bar, excited to order, and keen to return is to genuinely talk and listen to them, know when to ask questions, and know when to leave them alone.

"And it has to be real," he says. "We remember people's names, their drink preferences, their stories. We remember everything. And we do it because we want to."

When it comes to his cocktail list, Stroeve grew up in the country and has always had a strong connection to the land, and his drink-making is a conduit for that experience—communicating an image of Australia makes him proud.

WARATAH SPRITZ

THE WARATAH
308-310 LIVERPOOL ST, DARLINGHURST

In 2021, Evan Stroeve launched Australia's first commercial mistelle with business partners Tim Philips-Johansson and David Hobbs. RHUBI is a homage to traditional French mistelle, which is usually made from apples or pears. Evan uses Victorian and Tasmanian rhubarb to create his bittersweet, low-ABV aperitif. RHUBI is perfect in bubbly drinks such as the Waratah Spritz. You can substitute a cocktail syrup featuring lemon for the shrub, or experiment with other shrubs.

GLASSWARE: Wineglass

GARNISH: Lemon myrtle leaf or fresh citrus wedge

- 1⅓ oz. | 40 ml Yuzu Semillon (see recipe)
- ⅔ oz. | 20 ml RHUBI Mistelle
- ⅓ oz. | 10 ml Ziggy's Lilly

Pilly, Lemon Myrtle & Lavender Shrub
- 2⅔ oz. | 80 ml soda water

1. Add the Semillon, mistelle, shrub, and soda water to a wineglass over good quality ice.

2. Garnish with a lemon myrtle leaf or fresh citrus wedge.

YUZU SEMILLON
Peel 1 whole yuzu (10½ oz. | 300 grams), setting aside the skins. Slice the peeled yuzu into ⅕ in. (0.5 cm) wheels. Combine the yuzu wheels, yuzu peel, and 25⅓ oz. (750 ml) Semillon in a container and refrigerate overnight. The next day, strain the mixture through a sieve. The liquid will keep refrigerated for 1 month.

WATERMELON DAIQUIRI

PROMENADE
BONDI PAVILION, QUEEN ELIZABETH DR, BONDI BEACH

Tucked under the Spanish-inspired roof and historic arches of its heritage home at Bondi Pavilion is Promenade. Hospitality director Scott Brown says the inspiration for the venue was to create a space that felt elegant enough for a date night or celebratory occasion yet was also appealing to those who have just strolled off the beach. The Watermelon Daiquiri is "perfect for beachside summer drinking, and what fruit says, 'Aussie summer' better than fresh watermelon?"

GLASSWARE: Old-fashioned glass

GARNISH: Fresh watermelon wedge, chili salt

- 2 oz. | 60 ml fresh watermelon puree (2:1 watermelon juice to sugar)
- ½ oz. | 15 ml fresh lemon juice
- 1½ oz. | 45 ml white rum
- ⅔ oz. | 20 ml fresh strawberry puree
- Pinch salt

1. Chill an old-fashioned glass. In a blender, blend the ingredients with a small scoop of cracked ice.

2. Pour the cocktail into the chilled old-fashioned glass and top with a wedge of watermelon and a sprinkle of chili salt.

ARMY & NAVY

EILEEN'S BAR
410 CROWN ST, SURRY HILLS

Venue manager Gabriel Hepworth says the appeal of Eileen's is that it is a beautiful bar full of talented people who just want to chat about great gin and enjoy some really tasty drinks. "Locals love that we're a smaller, personable team with a big bar top for everybody to sit at, and visitors love finding smaller Four Pillars gins they may not have seen before. And the drinks are pretty bloody delicious too!" She has created this delicious take on the classic Army & Navy cocktail.

GLASSWARE: Nick & Nora glass

- 1$\frac{7}{20}$ oz. | 25 ml Four Pillars Navy Strength Gin
- 1$\frac{7}{20}$ oz. | 25 ml Four Pillars Modern Australian Gin
- $\frac{7}{10}$ oz. | 20 ml Macadamia Orgeat (see recipe, page 200)
- 1 teaspoon | 5 ml simple syrup
- Dash Angostura bitters
- Dash Angostura orange bitters

1. Chill a Nick & Nora glass. Add all of the ingredients to a cocktail shaker with ice.

2. Shake then fine-strain the cocktail into a frozen Nick & Nora.

MACADAMIA ORGEAT: Place 2 cups macadamias in a food processor and pulse until finely ground. Combine 1½ cups superfine (caster) sugar and 1¼ cups water in a medium saucepan and bring to the boil, stirring occasionally until the sugar dissolves. Reduce the heat and simmer for 3 to 4 minutes to reduce slightly. Add the macadamias and bring the mixture back to a boil. Turn off the heat, add ½ teaspoon orange flower water or blossoms, cover with a lid, and allow the mixture to stand for about 8 hours or overnight. Strain the orgeat through a fine strainer into a small bottle or jar.

EDUARDO CONDE,
EL PRIMO SANCHEZ

Put it down to the city's balmy weather or its residents' affection for spicy food, but Sydneysiders love their Mexican bars. One of the newest—and hottest—in town is El Primo Sanchez, a vibrant and colorful venue located in a historic 1940s pub on Oxford Street in Paddington. Its bar manager is Eduardo Conde, who relocated to Australia from Mexico almost a decade ago.

Conde's philosophy when it comes to bartending extends beyond what is in the glass. He believes that bartenders are starting to think beyond the bar and the drinks. According to him, bartenders are becoming more understanding that being a good person is more important than making a good drink. That means that working together and collaborating will always be the most important thing in a quality bartending career. As many patrons have never visited Mexico, he likes to take them on a sensory journey and explain the vision behind El Primo Sanchez.

THE CHAPALA CANTARITO

EL PRIMO SANCHEZ
27-33 OXFORD ST, PADDINGTON

Eduardo Conde was recently crowned the country's best bartender at the Diageo World Class Australian Finals. He expertly crafted a collection of superb cocktails, including a twist on an Old Fashioned featuring papaya and lemon geranium inspired by his Mexican heritage in a Johnnie Walker Blue Label challenge. Another of his winning serves was The Chapala Cantarito, featuring winter citrus. He suggests citrus cordial can be used as an alternative to kumquat oleo.

GLASSWARE: Ceramic vessel

- 2⅓ oz. | 70 ml citrus soda
- 1⅓ oz. | 40 ml Don Julio 1942
- 1 oz. | 30 ml mandarin juice
- ⅔ oz. | 20 ml kumquat oleo saccharum

1. Dry-shake the ingredients to combine in a cocktail shaker.

2. Pour the cocktail over ice and swizzle to serve.

SANCHEZ PALOMA

EL PRIMO SANCHEZ
27-33 OXFORD ST, PADDINGTON

With an interior color palette as vibrant as the backstreets of old Mexico City, the service of an internationally applauded bar team, a disco-ball dance floor, and a two-person karaoke booth, El Primo Sanchez is the kind of neighborhood bar we all wished we had. The drinks list at El Primo Sanchez is a collaborative effort led by Martin Hudak, Stefano Catino, and bar manager Eduardo Conde, with input from many of the Latin American staff who work there. Unsurprisingly, tequila and mezcal reign supreme, with the Sanchez Paloma being the signature cocktail.

GLASSWARE: Highball glass

GARNISH: Mandarin wedge

- 1 oz. | 30 ml tequila
- ½ oz. | 15 ml mandarin liqueur
- ⅓ oz. | 10 ml agave syrup
- 2⅔ oz. | 80 ml mandarin soda
- Salt, for the rim

1. Build up the ingredients—tequila, liqueur, syrup, then soda—in a salt-rimmed highball glass.

2. Garnish with a mandarin wedge.

FELICITY (FLICK) ESHMAN, SHADY PINES SALOON

Shady Pines Saloon has been channeling Nashville-style honky-tonk in inner-city Darlinghurst for almost ten years. Its admirers come for the laid-back pace, friendly welcome, and an eclectic atmosphere, which is enhanced by vintage taxidermy, a salvaged antique backbar, and a deep affection for good rye, Merle Haggard, Hank Williams, and the hard-living men of the highway.

Bar manager Felicity (Flick) Eshman has been at Shady Pines for more than three years and says the venue draws visitors from all over the world, who take a seat alongside regular faces each week.

Flick began her hospitality career in the city of Wollongong when she was eighteen, then moved to Sydney two years later. Her love for whiskey was born while working at the award-winning Baxter Inn before she joined Shady Pines Saloon. Her latest cocktail list at the bar showcases women she describes as "the most badass outlaws from the 1800s."

Three of the six cocktails in the selection highlight Flick's passion for whiskey: The Annie Oakley mixes rye whiskey, PX sherry, sweet vermouth, coconut, and chocolate bitters; the Goldie Griffith takes Tennessee whiskey and shakes it with white cacao, lychee, cinnamon, pineapple, and citrus; while the Calamity Jane highlights bourbon, mezcal, sweet vermouth, coffee, banana, and salt.

Her tip for the perfect cocktail serve is to ensure shaken drinks are handled correctly. This includes using the right amount of ice in the shaker, shaking for long enough, and also shaking hard and fast. Together, these actions combine, dilute, and aerate the cocktail correctly.

LOTTIE DENO

SHADY PINES SALOON
4/256 CROWN ST, DARLINGHURST

Carlotta J. Thompkins, also known as Lottie Deno, was a famous gambler in Texas and New Mexico known for her poker skills as well as her courage. Flick Eshman created an easy-drinking Spritz-style cocktail in Deno's name, which she describes as being "nothing short of delicious."

GLASSWARE: Wineglass

GARNISH: Sprig of rosemary

- 1¾ oz. | 50 ml sparkling wine
- 1½ oz. | 45 ml soda water
- ⅔ oz. | 20 ml gin
- ⅚ oz. | 25 ml Watermelon & Rose Syrup (see recipe)
- ½ oz. | 15 ml Lillet Blanc

1. Build the cocktail in a wineglass.

2. Add ice to the drink.

3. Garnish with a sprig of rosemary.

WATERMELON & ROSE SYRUP: In a medium saucepan over high heat, combine 2 cups watermelon juice, 2 cups sugar, and 3 drops rose water. When the mixture comes to a boil, reduce the heat to a simmer and simmer for 20 minutes, stirring until the sugar is dissolved. Strain before using or bottling.

PORNSTAR MARTINI

KANDI LUXE
120 BOURKE ST, WOOLLOOMOOLOO

Kandi Luxe has brought a touch of opulence to this working-class harborside suburb, with the added spice of burlesque-style entertainment on weekends. The Pornstar Martini reflects the essence of Sydney drinks culture, featuring fresh, sweet flavors and vibrant yellow hues. This Martini is best drunk from a coupe glass, so your hands don't warm the drink.

❖ ♣

GLASSWARE: Coupe glass
GARNISH: Fresh passion fruit half

- 1 oz. | 30 ml Belvedere Vodka
- 2 oz. | 60 ml Galliano Vanilla Liqueur
- 1 oz. | 30 ml passion fruit liqueur
- 2 oz. | 60 ml prosecco

1. Add all of the ingredients to a cocktail shaker with crushed ice.

2. Shake, then pour the drink through a strainer into a coupe glass.

3. Serve the cocktail garnished with a fresh passion fruit half.

PISCO SOUR

Nestled in the bustling culinary haven of Surry Hills lies Warike, a unique bar and restaurant fusing Peruvian and Mediterranean flavors. Warike's ambience is inspired by Peru's traditional "warikes"— humble, hidden eateries known for their incredible food and homely atmosphere. Pisco is the national drink of Peru, so it is hardly surprising that it is highlighted on the cocktail menu. Sydneysiders have taken the grape-distilled spirit to their hearts in recent years, with PROMPERÚ—the Commission for the Promotion of Peruvian Exports and Tourism—hosting regular cocktail-making competitions in the city to elevate awareness of the spirit.

GLASSWARE: Coupe glass

GARNISH: 4 drops Angostura bitters, dragged with a toothpick

- 1⅓ oz. | 35 ml fresh lime juice
- ⅚ oz. | 25 ml simple syrup
- ⅔ oz. | 20 ml triple sec
- 2⅕ oz. | 65 ml BarSol Pisco Quebranta
- ⅓ oz. | 10 ml aquafaba

1. Pour all of the ingredients in a cocktail shaker and dry-shake for 30 seconds.

2. Add ice and shake for another 10 seconds.

3. Double-strain the cocktail into a coupe glass.

4. To garnish, dot the surface of the liquid with Angostura bitters and drag with a toothpick, or to your liking.

SALTED CARAMEL RUM OLD FASHIONED

BRIX DISTILLERS BAR
350 BOURKE ST, SURRY HILLS

This bar within a working urban distillery offers guests the chance to see the distillers at work while sipping on a rum cocktail. Brix sits in the heart of Sydney's creative hub of Surry Hills and has sponsored the Sydney Film Festival for the past three years. The Salted Caramel Rum Old Fashioned was created for attendees seeking to sip something special before watching films. Brix co-founder James Christopher says a chilled glass and the perfect amount of ice are the keys to success for the cocktail. He suggests blending the ingredients together and tasting the drink until it reaches the perfect balance. A large ice cube will ensure the drink stays chilled but doesn't dilute too much.

GLASSWARE: Rocks glass

GARNISH: Caramel popcorn

- 2 oz. | 60 ml Brix Australian Rum
- ⅓ oz. | 10 ml salted caramel syrup
- 2 dashes chocolate bitters
- Dash orange bitters
- Orange peel, to express

1. Add all of the ingredients, except the orange peel, to a mixing glass.

2. Fill your mixing glass with ice and stir until you achieve the desired dilution, tasting as you stir.

3. Strain the cocktail into a rocks glass, preferably over a large block of ice.

4. Twist an orange peel over the finished cocktail to express its oils, discard the peel, and garnish with caramel popcorn.

YULEFEST RECORDS

CHISWICK WOOLLAHRA
65 OCEAN ST, WOOLLAHRA

Chiswick has been loved by Woollahra locals and visitors for more than a decade. Its garden setting and light, open cottage feel make the perfect setting for afternoon cocktails. Chiswick is known for its Spritzes, which change flavors with the seasons. The Yulefest Records pays homage to long, refreshing drinks of summer that Sydneysiders love, no matter the weather.

GLASSWARE: Plumm no. 2 wineglass

GARNISH: 2 fresh sage leaves, powdered sugar

- 1 oz. | 30 ml Royal Gala Cordial (see recipe)
- 1 oz. | 30 ml prosecco
- 1 oz. | 30 ml soda water
- ½ oz. | 15 ml fresh lime juice
- ⅔ oz. | 20 ml Grey Goose Vodka
- ⅓ oz. | 10 ml Villa Massa Limoncello

1. Build all of the ingredients in a wineglass.

2. Top up with ice, then garnish with 2 sage leaves.

3. Dust powdered sugar on top of the leaves to create a "snow" effect.

ROYAL GALA CORDIAL:

In a pot, bring 10 oz. (300 ml) water to a boil. Reduce the heat to a simmer, then add ⅙ oz. (5 grams) cinnamon stick and ¼4 oz. (2 grams) star anise and simmer for 5 minutes. Remove the solids and dissolve 2½ cups (500 grams) sugar and ½ teaspoon salt in the liquid mixture. Place the liquid in the refrigerator to chill. Remove the seeds and stems from 7 oz. (200 grams) Royal Gala apples. Blend the apples (skin on). Add some syrup before blending so that the apples don't damage your blender. This needs to be done quickly so the apples don't go brown (you can add ascorbic acid and some syrup to prevent browning). Combine the syrup and apple puree, then strain. Add ½ teaspoon of ascorbic acid to the final product to prevent oxidation. Keep chilled.

COCO BONGO

One of the biggest draws of North Bondi Fish is its amazing location, which overlooks the world-famous Bondi Beach. The Coco Bongo is a twist on the Spicy Marg and was inspired by the popular Riviera Maya beach snack of spicy coconut with lime juice. Tequila—which might just be the favorite spirit in Sydney's East—was also key in making this cocktail a North Bondi Fish classic. The touch of nature from the samphire, mixed with the spicy notes, gives this drink its Sydney essence.

GLASSWARE: Rocks glass

GARNISH: Pandan leaf, whole dried chile pepper

- 1½ oz. | 45 ml Samphire-Infused Tequila (see recipe)
- 1 oz. | 30 ml l fresh lime juice
- ½ oz. | 15 ml triple sec
- ½ oz. | 15 ml coconut syrup
- 3 dashes habanero tincture

1. Add all the ingredients to a cocktail shaker with ice and shake well.

2. Finely strain the mixture into a rocks glass

3. Garnish the drink with a pandan leaf and a whole dried chile.

SAMPHIRE-INFUSED TEQUILA: In a saucepan, slowly warm up a mixture of 1 bottle of Patrón Silver Tequila, the peel of half an orange, ⅓ oz. (10 grams) samphire, and one pandan leaf. Do not allow the mixture to boil. Keep the liquid warming for 30 minutes. Remove it from heat and leave it to rest for 12 hours before using.

JULEP RE-FASHIONED

PARLAR
SHOP 3/81 MACLEAY ST, ELIZABETH BAY

In the summer months, guests at Parlar take advantage of the breezy terrace, while the cozy dining room is beloved when the cold comes. The Julep Re-Fashioned mixes local brandy with a touch of mint and a little spice from ginger, all wrapped around a crystal-clear ice cube. It also calls for quality sherry and ice. Importantly, give that mint sprig a slap to release its essence before you insert it between the glass and the ice cube.

GLASSWARE: Heavy-based whiskey tumbler

GARNISH: Mint sprigs

- 1½ oz. | 45 ml ginger-infused 23rd St Not Your Nanna's Brandy
- ⅔ oz. | 20 ml amontillado sherry
- ½ oz. | 15 ml Mint-Infused Simple Syrup (see recipe)
- 2 dashes Angostura bitters

1. Stir all of the ingredients together in a mixing glass over ice until chilled and slightly diluted.

2. Strain the cocktail over a large cube of ice into a heavy-based whiskey tumbler.

3. Garnish with a couple of sprigs of mint perched between the ice and the edge of the glass.

MINT-INFUSED SIMPLE SYRUP: Dissolve 10 oz. (300 grams) sugar in 10 oz. (300 ml) water until the water is clear. Place the simple syrup in a large French press. Add 2 cups of fresh mint leaves, set the lid on top, and refrigerate overnight. Plunge the mint leaves the next day and bottle the liquid.

ELECTRIC MARGARITA

FRANCA
SHOP 2/81 MACLEAY ST, POTTS POINT

Sydney's warm climate makes Margaritas a popular choice at Franca. Szechuan pepper adds complexity and depth of flavor to the bar's Electric Margarita, which is balanced out by the sweetness of the watermelon and a punch of acid from the freshly squeezed lime.

GLASSWARE: Double rocks glass
GARNISH: Reamed lime half, watermelon ball

- 1¾ oz. | 50 ml Szechuan Pepper–Infused Tequila (see recipe)
- ⅔ oz. | 20 ml Watermelon Cordial (see recipe)
- ⅔ oz. | 20 ml fresh lime juice

1. Add all of the ingredients to a cocktail shaker with ice and shake.

2. Double-strain the cocktail into a double rocks glass.

3. Garnish with reamed lime half and watermelon ball.

SZECHUAN PEPPER–INFUSED TEQUILA: Add 2 tablespoons of Szechuan peppercorns to 1 bottle of Volcan De Mi Tierra Blanco Tequila (or any other premium blanco tequila). Let the infusion sit for 8 hours, then strain.

WATERMELON CORDIAL: Juice a fresh watermelon, then cut it with sugar in a 1:1 ratio of watermelon juice and sugar.

SHIRAZ ME NOT

THE WINERY
285A CROWN ST, SURRY HILLS

The Winery is an enchanting and delightfully eccentric urban wine bar, with a lush laneway entrance and a terrace that invites guests to bask in the warmth of the sun. As dusk falls, a captivating scene beckons patrons to drink and dine under the twinkling fairy lights. Assistant venue manager Milos Jovic says the bar's signature cocktail, the Shiraz Me Not, seamlessly combines a medley of ingredients that possess individual brilliance, yet harmoniously unite to create a well-balanced cocktail. Infusing a favorite Shiraz with jelly powder—vegan-friendly agar agar is ideal—creates miniature bursts of flavor called Shiraz caviar. While not essential to the cocktail, these spheres add a playful touch, enhancing the overall experience of the drink.

GLASSWARE: Highball glass
GARNISH: Shiraz Caviar (see recipe)

- ⅔ oz. | 20 ml Four Pillars Bloody Shiraz Gin
- ⅔ oz. | 20 ml Ketel One Citroen
- ⅔ oz. | 20 ml Licor 43
- ½ oz. | 15 ml cranberry juice
- ½ oz. | 15 ml pineapple juice
- ½ oz. | 15 ml fresh lemon juice
- ⅓ oz. | 10 ml orgeat
- Skinny barspoon edible lilac luster powder

1. Add all of the ingredients to a cocktail shaker and shake with ice.

2. Strain the cocktail into a highball glass.

3. Garnish with Shiraz caviar.

SHIRAZ CAVIAR: Infuse a bottle of your favorite Shiraz with agar agar (or other jelly powder) as needed to achieve a caviar-like consistency.

CAMPARI FRAISE

ARMORICA
SHOP 1 & 2/490 CROWN ST, SURRY HILLS

Guests are transported to a modern Parisian brasserie when they step inside Armorica. The Harbour City is renowned for its mild weather and the Campari Fraise cocktail has been created to be refreshing and vibrant, much like a sunny Sydney day.

GLASSWARE: Coupe glass

GARNISH: 3 dots of olive oil

- 2 oz. | 60 ml Campari Strawberry Infusion (see recipe)
- ½ oz. | 15 ml fresh lemon juice
- ½ oz. | 15 ml simple syrup
- 2 dashes saline solution

1. Chill a coupe glass. Shake all of the ingredients together in a cocktail shaker with ice.

2. Double-strain the cocktail into the chilled coupe.

3. Garnish with 3 olive oil dots.

CAMPARI STRAWBERRY INFUSION: Remove the stems from 21⅛ oz. (600 grams) fresh strawberries and cut the strawberries into halves. Combine the strawberries and 23⅔ oz. (700 ml) Campari in a jar and leave to infuse at room temperature for 48 hours. Strain, bottle, label, and refrigerate the infusion.

WATERMELON SUGAR

TAQIZA
79 HALL ST, BONDI BEACH

Translating as "taco party" in Spanish, Taqiza offers contemporary taco combinations paired with mezcals and agave spirits. The cocktail list is curated by head bartender Luna Ercoli and aims to utilize produce featured in Australia and Mexico, with a twist on traditional cocktail combinations. The Watermelon Sugar is a frozen Margarita with a nutty aftertaste that comes from the inclusion of pandan cordial, which is created from the Southeast Asian pandan plant's leaves.

GLASSWARE: Coupe glass

GARNISH: 2 pandan leaves

- 1⅓ oz. | 40 ml Watermelon & Pandan Cordial (see recipe)
- 1 oz. | 30 ml blanco tequila
- ⅚ oz. | 25 ml simple syrup
- ½ oz. | 15 ml raicilla

1. Place all of the ingredients in a blender with one scoop of ice and blend.

2. Pour the cocktail into a coupe and garnish with 2 pandan leaves.

WATERMELON & PANDAN CORDIAL: Blend 25⅓ oz. (750 ml) watermelon juice with 10 drops pandan extract and ⅙ oz. (5 grams) citric acid.

SANDPRINT

Coogee is home to a fun, come-as-you-are drinks scene. Based on the middle floor of Coogee Pavilion facing the beach, Will's features stunning views, attentive staff, and world-class drinks. The bar staff say there are no real secrets to making the Sandprint, just the golden rules you follow with any cocktail—fresh ingredients, ice-cold glass, and the correct technique to ensure the best possible drink. In this case, total emulsification of the liquid is a must.

GLASSWARE: Coupe glass
GARNISH: Toasted buckwheat

- 1½ oz. | 45 ml pandan-infused vodka
- 1 oz. | 30 ml fresh pineapple juice
- ½ oz. | 15 ml horchata syrup
- ¹⁄₃₂ oz. | 1 ml fino sherry
- Dash aquafaba

1. Chill a coupe glass. In a cocktail shaker, reverse dry-shake all of the ingredients: first shake with ice, then strain the liquid and shake again, this time without ice.

2. Fine-strain the cocktail into the chilled coupe.

3. Garnish with a scattering of toasted buckwheat.

PLEASE & THANK YOU

THE BUTLER
123 VICTORIA ST, POTTS POINT

This is a cocktail that has stood the test of time at The Butler at Potts Point and for good reason. A unique balance of lemon, grapefruit, lychee, and vanilla makes up the body of this gin-and-elderflower-based drink, which is served with a garnish of baby's breath flowers. Bar manager Matt Johnson says Sydneysiders have come to recognize this signature serve as an integral part of The Butler's identity, so although it has undergone subtle changes and iterations over the years, it stays on the menu. It makes for a perfect sipper while enjoying The Butler's iconic city skyline view. The secret to a perfect serve, says Matt, is the thin layer of foam across the top, so the delicate branch of flowers appears to be blossoming from out of the drink.

GLASSWARE: Coupe glass
GARNISH: Baby's breath flowers

- 1 oz. | 30 ml gin
- 1 oz. | 30 ml fresh lemon juice
- 1 oz. | 30 ml grapefruit juice
- ½ oz. | 15 ml elderflower liqueur
- ½ oz. | 15 ml lychee vanilla syrup
- 10 ml aquafaba

1. Add all of the ingredients to a cocktail shaker and shake with ice.

2. Double-strain the cocktail into a coupe.

3. Garnish with baby's breath flowers so they appear to blossom out from the drink.

FORRY'S BLOODY MARY

FORRESTER'S
336 RILEY ST, SURRY HILLS

Forrester's bar manager Sam Glickman says there's nothing like a Forry's Bloody Mary "to steady the ship" after a big night out. The secret is in the homemade Bloody Mary mix that the bar has spent the past couple years perfecting. He's keeping his recipe under wraps, but suggests experimenting with making your own with popular ingredients like tomato juice, horseradish, lemon juice, Worcestershire sauce, black pepper, sea salt, and celery salt. Sam describes Forrester's as the ultimate "local," with live music, sports, a cozy atmosphere, and friendly staff. "You can't beat it. It's dog friendly and has the best roast dinner in Sydney."

GLASSWARE: Collins glass
GARNISH: 2 cocktail onions, olive, lemon, rosemary sprig

- Chili salt, for the rim
- 3 oz. | 90 ml fresh tomato juice
- 1 oz. | 30 ml Bloody Mary mix
- 1½ oz. | 45 ml gin, vodka, or tequila
- Dash hot sauce

1. Coat the rim of a collins glass with chili salt.

2. Build the cocktail in the glass and garnish with 2 cocktail onions, an olive, lemon, and rosemary sprig.

CARLOTTA

THE ROOSEVELT
32 ORWELL ST, POTTS POINT

The Carlotta is a tribute to the most famous dancer in Les Girls, a famous all-male revue cabaret show in Kings Cross that drew audiences from around the globe. She eventually became known as "The Queen of The Cross" as the show's host. Although best known as a cabaret performer, Carlotta also appeared on an Australian television series in 1974 called *Number 96* as Miss Robyn Ross. It was the first time worldwide that a transgender character was portrayed by a transgender actor on screen. According to The Roosevelt's general manager Ben Hickey, cocktails should be visually appealing as well as taste amazing. Having attractive glassware that is the right size for the volume of the cocktail and a garnish that complements the drink are very important. "We garnish the Carlotta with a small blueberry and meringue tart, but you can just use some fresh blueberries and a sage leaf." If you want, you can lemon-infuse your own vodka at home.

GLASSWARE: Coupe glass

GARNISH: Fresh blueberries, fresh sage leaf

- 2 oz. | 60 ml lemon vodka
- 1 oz. | 30 ml fresh lemon juice
- 1 oz. | 30 ml Blueberry, Thyme, and Sage Syrup (see recipe)
- ⅓ oz. | 10 ml egg white or liquid foam
- 3 dashes rhubarb bitters

1. Combine all of the ingredients in a cocktail shaker.

2. Dry-shake without ice, then shake again with a cocktail shaker full of ice.

3. Strain the cocktail through a fine-mesh strainer into a coupe.

4. Garnish with blueberries and a sage leaf.

BLUEBERRY, THYME, AND SAGE SYRUP: Cook 2⅕ lbs. (1 kg) frozen blueberries, 2⅕ lbs. (1 kg) granulated sugar, 1 bunch of thyme, and 1 bunch of sage together with 4¼ cups (1 liter) water in a saucepan on low heat without boiling. Remove the pan from heat and allow the mixture to cool. Strain the ingredients through a mesh strainer and press the solids to extract all the liquid. Add 3⅔ oz. (100 ml) vodka and bottle the syrup. The syrup will keep in the refrigerator for 2 weeks.

SOUTH
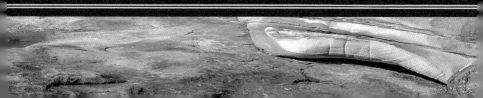

NIGHT AT THE ROSEBERY

THE FLAMIN GALAH

FRENCHIES NEGRONI

THE TULIP

BLACK SESAME ICE CREAM
NEGRONI

FRUIT DE LA PASSION

NORTHERN NIGHTS

Sydney's South offers an eclectic mix of industry, history, and stunning beaches. Its landscape varies from Botany Bay, where British explorer Captain James Cook landed in 1770, to industrial warehouses, the oldest national park in Australia, and wide stretches of white beaches.

In recent years, the region has also become home to destination bars such as Archie Rose and The Grounds, which have sprung up among the warehouses in the mixed-use enclaves of Rosebery and Alexandria.

The Grounds is a sprawling cafe, restaurant, bar, coffee roastery, bakery, florist, market, and farm all in one. Nestled in a former pie factory, its lush, fantasy decor—at odds with the former industrial location—has led it to become one of the most Instagrammable spots in the city.

Five minutes away, Archie Rose Bar is flanked by a distillery and a wall of whiskey casks, offering an atmospheric place to pull up a stool and enjoy award-winning spirits alongside a varied selection of local and global spirits, craft beers, wine, and food by local producers.

If you prefer to sip your cocktails by the sea, explore the Cronulla Beach bar scene and enjoy libations while drinking in the views.

GEOFF FEWELL, ARCHIE ROSE BAR

85 DUNNING AVE, ROSEBERY

Bars such as Archie Rose have been springing up among the warehouses in the industrial hubs of Rosebery and Alexandria. Archie Rose spirits are quintessentially Australian, with the distillers choosing to highlight native ingredients in their botanicals, malts, cocktail ingredients, and garnishes. A ground floor area and a mezzanine use copper, steel, oak, and concrete to create a striking space where visitors can sample, sip, and savor world-class cocktails.

Venue manager Geoff Fewell, who has been described as a "long-time bar wizard" by *Australian Bartender* magazine, has worked at some of the best bars in Canberra and Sydney during his career. After recently joining Archie Rose, he is creating magic by mixing cocktails featuring Archie Rose spirits. Fewell says there's nothing like savoring a quality cocktail just steps away from the stills that created the spirits that lie at the heart of the drinks.

NIGHT AT THE ROSEBERY

ARCHIE ROSE BAR
85 DUNNING AVE, ROSEBERY

One of Archie Rose Bar's top-selling cocktails is Night at the Rosebery, highlighting its Distiller's Strength Gin combined with watermelon, strawberry, and citrus. The gin features honey from Archie Rose's own beehives, plus NSW pear, rose, and elderflower. While the cocktail is not on the bar's winter menu, it returns for spring. However, venue manager Geoff Fewell says patrons can ask the bartenders to make it for them at any time of year. Should Archie Rose spirits not be available for use in your home bar, Fewell suggests substituting your favorite distiller's strength gin.

GLASSWARE: Collins glass

- 1⅓ oz. | 40 ml Archie Rose Distiller's Strength Gin
- ⅔ oz. | 20 ml fresh lemon juice
- ½ oz. | 15 ml egg white
- Dash rose water
- ⅓ oz. | 10 ml watermelon juice
- 1 oz. | 30 ml strawberry syrup
- Soda water, to top

1. Add all of the ingredients to a cocktail shaker, except for the soda water.

2. Dry- and wet-shake—shake once with no ice, and then again with ice.

3. Fine-strain the drink over ice into a collins glass.

4. Top with a splash of soda water.

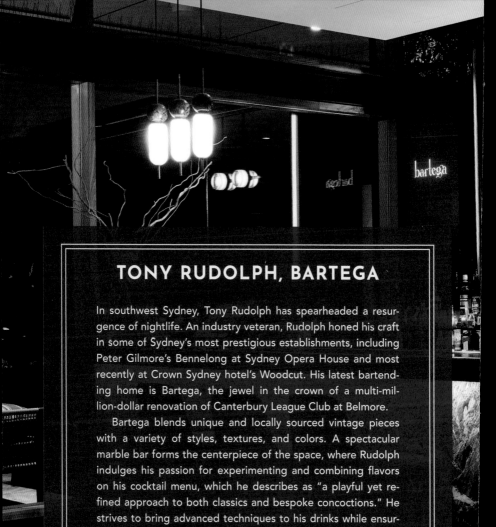

TONY RUDOLPH, BARTEGA

In southwest Sydney, Tony Rudolph has spearheaded a resurgence of nightlife. An industry veteran, Rudolph honed his craft in some of Sydney's most prestigious establishments, including Peter Gilmore's Bennelong at Sydney Opera House and most recently at Crown Sydney hotel's Woodcut. His latest bartending home is Bartega, the jewel in the crown of a multi-million-dollar renovation of Canterbury League Club at Belmore.

Bartega blends unique and locally sourced vintage pieces with a variety of styles, textures, and colors. A spectacular marble bar forms the centerpiece of the space, where Rudolph indulges his passion for experimenting and combining flavors on his cocktail menu, which he describes as "a playful yet refined approach to both classics and bespoke concoctions." He strives to bring advanced techniques to his drinks while ensuring they remain approachable. An example is the technique of "suppression," a freezing method pioneered by a bar in the United Kingdom called Panda & Sons that involves using semi-defrosted concentrated juice in cocktails, providing a significantly enhanced flavor.

THE FLAMIN GALAH

BARTEGA
CANTERBURY LEAGUE CLUB, 26 BRIDGE RD, BELMORE

The Flamin Galah is Bartega's twist on the classic Jungle Bird cocktail created in Singapore in the 1960s. What makes Bartega's version unique is the blend of spiced rum, Campari, pineapple juice, and lime, coupled with the bar's specialty, pineapple-flavored ice. This ice, along with smoked cinnamon over the top, lends a texture to the drink that is similar to a Piña Colada. The presentation mirrors an Australian native bird called the galah, which is famous for its pink colors and white feathered head. Bartega uses a Queensland craft rum called Kalki Moon, but any craft spiced rum can be substituted.

GLASSWARE: Hurricane glass

GARNISH: Galah Presentation (see recipe)

- Pineapple-flavored ice cubes, as needed
- 1 oz. | 30 ml Campari
- 1 oz. | 30 ml fresh lime juice
- 2 oz. | 60 ml Kalki Moon Spiced Rum
- 3 oz. | 90 ml fresh pineapple juice

1. Fill a blender with pineapple-flavored ice cubes.

2. Add the remaining ingredients to the blender and blend until the mixture is smooth, similar to the consistency of a Piña Colada.

3. Pour the cocktail into a hurricane glass and add the garnishes.

GALAH PRESENTATION:

Using a blowtorch, lightly scorch some cinnamon over the top of the cocktail to add a hint of smoky flavor. Once the cinnamon is added, place the lime half on top. The lime will start sparking, due to the interaction between the heat from the cinnamon and the citrus oils in the lime peel. This adds to the "flaming" spectacle of the cocktail. Garnish the cocktail with 3 pineapple fronds to create the effect of a galah's crest. Finally, take a second lime half, scoop out the inside to create a "cup," place it on top of the cocktail, and add a small amount of high-proof rum (about ⅙ to ⅓ oz. | 5 to 10 ml). Light it up carefully to complete the flaming garnish. Extinguish the flame before drinking.

FRENCHIES NEGRONI

FRENCHIES BISTRO & BREWERY
6/61-71 MENTMORE AVE, ROSEBERY

Sydneysiders love the classic Negroni. Ours is made in small batches on a regular basis and available on tap," venue manager Charly Ben Azouz says. "This approach proves popular with customers due to the theatricality of it and its flavorsome nature. We also pair our Negroni with blood orange in the warmer months, so it's a popular tipple all year round."

GLASSWARE: Short whiskey glass

GARNISH: Orange slice

- 1 oz. | 30 ml Dolin Bitter
- 1 oz. | 30 ml Dubonnet Rouge Grand Aperitif de France
- 1 oz. | 30 ml Le Gin de Christian Drouin
- Dash bitters

1. Pour all of the ingredients, except for the bitters, into a mixing glass with ice.

2. Stir, then strain the cocktail into a short whiskey glass with fresh ice.

3. Add a dash of bitters and garnish with an orange slice.

THE TULIP

RE
2 LOCOMOTIVE ST, EVELEIGH

Evan Stroeve created The Tulip in 2021 when he won Australian Bartender of the Year and went on to represent Australia at the Global World Class competition. During one of the cocktail challenges, he was tasked with creating a drink that connected with the community around him. The Tulip uses produce sourced exclusively from farms on the outskirts of Sydney, as well as pink peppercorn and lemon myrtle—plants that frame many Sydney streets. The Tulip is akin to a Martini and Evan says the trick to the perfect Martini is dilution and temperature. He advises that stirring the drink for 30 seconds should "land you in a pretty happy place."

GLASSWARE: Tulip wineglass

GARNISH: Lemon twist

- 1½ oz. | 45 ml Ketel One Vodka
- ⅚ oz. | 25 ml Apple Butter Verjus (see recipe)
- 5 drops saline solution
- 1 teaspoon | 5 ml white crème de cacao
- 5 drops Pink Peppercorn Vinegar (see recipe)

1. Add all of the ingredients to a mixing glass over good quality ice.

2. Stir the drink for 30 seconds.

3. Strain the cocktail into a tulip wineglass.

4. Garnish with a lemon twist.

APPLE BUTTER VERJUS: Slice a green apple thinly, or use a mandolin. You need 8½ oz. (700 grams) of green apple. Melt 17½ oz. (500 grams) uncultured butter over a low heat. Add 8½ oz. (700 ml) chardonnay verjus and the apple to the butter and cook on low for 30 minutes. Transfer the mixture to a Tupperware container and refrigerate overnight. By the time you come back in the morning, the butter should have solidified, allowing you to strain off the clear apple butter verjus.

PINK PEPPERCORN VINEGAR: Add 17½ oz. (500 ml) apple cider vinegar and 3½ oz. (100 grams) fresh pink peppercorns to a blender and blend until smooth. Strain out the solids and retain the flavored peppercorn vinegar.

BLACK SESAME ICE CREAM NEGRONI

PAPA JS
SHOP 7/2/6 CRONULLA ST, CRONULLA

Papa Js is an intimate bar located in the beachside suburb of Cronulla, around an hour from Sydney's CBD. This cocktail was inspired by dinner at a Japanese restaurant. "My son was having black sesame ice cream for dessert, and I was having a Negroni," says bar manager Josh Metcalfe. "As I was trying both, the idea was born to infuse the two very different flavors together." Papa Js uses Papa Js x Chronicles Gin.

GLASSWARE: Lowball glass

GARNISH: Black sesame cracker

- 1½ oz. | 45 ml Black Sesame Ice Cream Gin (see recipe)
- ⅓ oz. | 10 ml Campari
- ½ oz. | 15 ml Regal Rogue Bold Red Vermouth

1. In a mixing glass, stir all of the ingredients with ice.

2. Single-strain the drink over a large ice cube into a lowball glass.

3. Lay a black sesame cracker on top of the ice cube for garnish.

BLACK SESAME ICE CREAM GIN: Infuse 23½ oz. (700 ml) gin with 3½ oz. (100 grams) black sesame paste and 10 oz. (300 ml) filtered water overnight. Use a rotary evaporator to extract the gin from the infusion. Stir in ½ oz. (4 grams) lactose until dissolved.

FRUIT DE LA PASSION

THE POTTING SHED
41/43 BOURKE RD, ALEXANDRIA

T he best way to make a perfect cocktail is to practice, practice, practice," says Ramzey Choker, founder of The Potting Shed at The Grounds of Alexandria. His magical bar is located inside the remnants of a heritage-listed warehouse where a pie factory once stood. The décor was inspired by Choker's experience of sitting "out the back" at his grandparents' house with friends, relaxing on the porch steps surrounded by stories, laughter, and a rambling garden. The Fruit De La Passion has a distinctly local flavor, using vodka from Sydney artisan distiller Mobius Distilling Co, which is based down the road in Marrickville.

GLASSWARE: Coupe glass
GARNISH: ½ passion fruit, passion fruit flower

- 1½ oz. | 45 ml Mobius 38 Special Vodka
- ⅔ oz. | 20 ml simple syrup
- 2 oz. | 60 ml pineapple juice
- 1 oz. | 30 ml passion fruit pulp
- ⅔ oz. | 20 ml fresh lemon juice

1. Chill a coupe glass. Build the drink by adding all of the ingredients to a cocktail shaker and shake over ice.

2. Double-strain the cocktail into the chilled coupe.

NORTHERN NIGHTS

MJØLNER
267 CLEVELAND ST, REDFERN

Mjølner is a luxe Viking- and Norse-inspired bar and restaurant featuring a contemporary Scandinavian design. According to the bar team, Sydneysiders always lean into light, fresh tipples to manage the warmer months. Northern Lights combines iced Riesling and gin—the perfect marriage of a crisp white and a Gin and Tonic, the best of both worlds.

GLASSWARE: Tall wineglass
GARNISH: Sorrel leaf, pickled grape

- 1⅓ oz. | 40 ml Beefeater Gin
- ⁹⁄₁₀ oz. | 27.5 ml ice Riesling

- ⅔ oz. | 20 ml sorrel and elderflower cordial
- ¼ oz. | 7.5 ml Malic Acid Solution (see recipe)

1. In a tall wineglass, combine all of the ingredients and churn thoroughly with crushed ice.

2. Garnish with a sorrel leaf and pickled grape and serve with a metal straw.

MALIC ACID SOLUTION: In a container, combine 3 ⅓ oz. (100 ml) water and 10 grams malic acid powder. Whisk to dissolve the powder and bottle.

Nick & Nora's

WEST

HILLS HOIST

LA PERLA NEGRA

RAMOS GIN FIZZ

CANE OF THE CROP

THE F**KTINI

COASTAL NEGRONI

CARLA'S MARTINI

THE DRUNKEN BOTANIST

SOUR NEGRONI

CARDINALE SIN

While Sydney's harbor is the image that first comes to mind when thinking of the city, its heart actually lies almost fifteen miles—twenty-four km—west, in Parramatta. The suburbs surrounding the hubs of Parramatta and Penrith feature a lively restaurant, bar, and arts and culture scene.

Closer to Sydney CBD, the Inner West transformed into one of Sydney's most thriving entertainment hubs following the introduction of lockout laws to the inner city in 2014. The laws were in force from 2014 to 2020, with bars not allowed to admit patrons after 1:30 a.m. and last drinks being called at 3 a.m. Sydneysiders went west seeking entertainment, which breathed new life into the region's bar scene, clustered along King Street and Enmore Road.

Must-visit bohemian neighborhoods in the Inner West include Newtown, Enmore, and Marrickville. Expect a relaxing atmosphere, loads of live music, and clusters of cool bars along King Street and Enmore Road.

LIAM DOHERTY-PENZER, THE BOB HAWKE BEER & LEISURE CENTRE

Slightly farther afield in Marrickville's industrial precinct lies The Bob Hawke Beer & Leisure Centre, named after Australia's most famous prime minister. The bar is as much a tribute to the late politician as it is a love letter to Australiana and the coziness of familiarity, with areas like The Public Bar, The Pool Room, and The Patio setting the stage on entry. There is also the Australian Chinese bistro The Lucky Prawn, which echoes the quintessential 1980s pub and community club experience.

The focus at The Bob Hawke Beer & Leisure Centre may be on beer, but its drinks list has grown to include an irreverent cocktail menu created by Liam Doherty-Penzer. Liam has worked at Sydney bar favorites The Rook, Whirly Bird, and The Barber Shop. Many of his creations include Asian ingredients, designed to pair with the specialties on the menu at The Lucky Prawn restaurant and echo the many ethnic eateries in surrounding Marrickville.

HILLS HOIST

THE BOB HAWKE BEER & LEISURE CENTRE
8-12 SYDNEY ST, MARRICKVILLE

Liam Doherty-Penzer's Hills Hoist cocktail is named after the iconic Australian rotary clothesline. Creating a balance between all ingredients is always key, he says: you don't want the spice from the pepper and the tartness from the strawberries to overpower the rest of the ingredients. Using plenty of ice is another of his top tips.

GLASSWARE: Highball glass
GARNISH: Lemon wheel(s)

- 1⅓ oz. | 40 ml Hickson Rd. Australian Dry Gin
- ⅔ oz. | 20 ml Strawberry-and-Szechuan-Pepper Syrup (see recipe)
- ⅔ oz. | 20 ml Aperol

- ⅔ oz. | 20 ml fresh lemon juice
- 2 dashes Peychaud's bitters
- Yuzu soda, to top

1. Wet-shake all of the ingredients, except for the yuzu soda, with ice in a cocktail shaker.

2. Strain the cocktail into a highball.

3. Top with yuzu soda and garnish with a lemon wheel.

STRAWBERRY-AND-SZECHUAN-PEPPER SYRUP: Add 1 pound (500 grams) strawberries, hulled and chopped; the zest and juice of 2 lemons, 1 teaspoon ground Sichuan pepper, and ½ teaspoon salt to a food processor and blitz to combine. Pour the mixture into a medium saucepan and add 1 cup superfine (caster) sugar and 1 star anise pod. Bring the mixture gently to a boil, lower the heat, and simmer for 20 to 25 minutes, until the mixture is jam-like. Strain the syrup through a fine-mesh sieve before using or storing.

QUINTON SEETO, BABY DRAGON BAR

Baby Dragon Bar lies a few doors down from Art Deco landmark the Enmore Theatre, a legendary Inner West location for live music and comedy gigs. The bar's fantasy décor is a million miles away from the historic elegance of its stately neighbor: Baby Dragon is filled with rocks, waterfalls, vines, a towering cherry blossom tree, and an equally out-of-this-world cocktail list.

Resident mixologist Quinton Seeto has spent more than twenty-five years in the industry, honing his skills at dive bars, pubs, fine-dining restaurants, and five-star hotels around the world. Along the way he has learned that most people drink with their eyes, so his creations seamlessly combine exquisite flavor with theatrics such as smoke and flames. Seeto provides customers with a theatrical experience unlike any other offered in Sydney, and each drink on his cocktail menu comes with its own QR code. When scanned, it shows the drink being created to ensure every guest can still get the full experience, even when not sitting at the bar. While the theatrics keep patrons' social media feeds happy, Seeto's expertly balanced cocktails ensure tastebuds are equally satisfied.

LA PERLA NEGRA

BABY DRAGON BAR 112 ENMORE RD, NEWTOWN

U nlike many of Quinton Seeto's more theatrical creations, La Perla Negra's explosive flavors are its only spectacle. At the heart of the drink is gin. Quinton's favorite choice is the big, bold, juniper- and citrus-forward Sipsmith London Dry. The cocktail also features tart blackberry puree and tangy lemon juice, which Quinton squeezes fresh daily. House-made rose syrup and lemongrass and kaffir lime syrup elevate the experience further. The addition of aquafaba brings a slight saltiness to the drink, which awakens the tastebuds and creates a meringue-like texture that complements the grittiness of the activated charcoal.

GLASSWARE: Brandy balloon glass

GARNISH: Edible flower

- 1½ oz. | 45 ml Sipsmith London Dry Gin
- 1 oz. | 30 ml fresh lemon juice
- ⅔ oz. | 20 ml blackberry puree
- ½ oz. | 15 ml rose syrup
- ½ oz. | 15 ml Lemongrass & Kaffir Lime Syrup (see recipe)
- ½ oz. | 15 ml aquafaba (or egg white)
- ½ barspoon activated charcoal

1. Combine all of the ingredients, except the activated charcoal, in a cocktail shaker and dry-shake hard to activate the aquafaba.

2. Add ice and the activated charcoal and shake well.

3. Fine-strain the cocktail into a brandy balloon glass. Garnish with an edible flower.

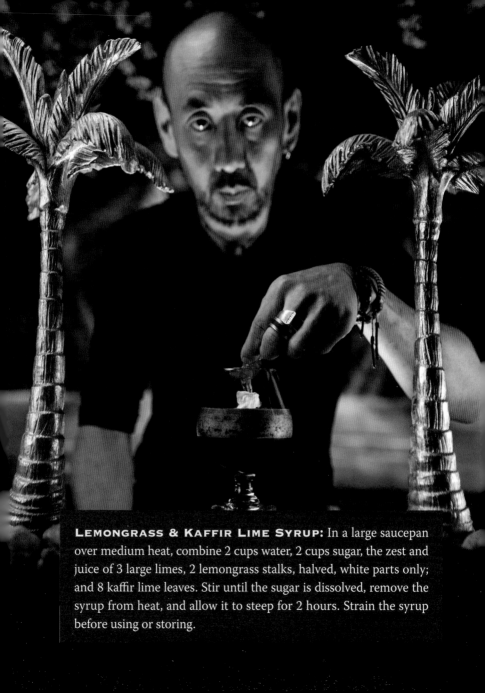

LEMONGRASS & KAFFIR LIME SYRUP: In a large saucepan over medium heat, combine 2 cups water, 2 cups sugar, the zest and juice of 3 large limes, 2 lemongrass stalks, halved, white parts only; and 8 kaffir lime leaves. Stir until the sugar is dissolved, remove the syrup from heat, and allow it to steep for 2 hours. Strain the syrup before using or storing.

RAMOS GIN FIZZ

CONTINENTAL DELICATESSEN
210 AUSTRALIA ST, NEWTOWN

Continental Delicatessen opened its doors in 2015 and immediately captivated Sydneysiders by canning everything from salted caramel to cocktails. Its iconic Mar-Tinny has been served at the bar since day one, with co-owner Michael Nicolian crediting the canned creation with reviving the city's affection for Martinis. According to Nicolian, Sydneysiders had almost forgotten the Martini existed, but in the last seven years it has returned to the forefront of bartending in the city. Aside from the Mar-Tinny, the Continental's cocktail list focuses on the classics—the Americano, Negroni, and the Ramos Gin Fizz, which Nicolian describes as being "the best in town." Nicolian says many cocktail bartenders don't like to make the Ramos as they mistakenly believe it has to be shaken too hard. He insists that is not the case and if you stick to the rules—use a chilled glass with straight edges and icy cold soda, pour, then wait for a minute before topping up—you will get the rise that makes the drink so special.

GLASSWARE: Collins glass

- 1¾ oz. | 50 ml gin
- ⅔ oz. | 20 ml cream
- ⅔ oz. | 20 ml egg white
- ½ oz. | 15 ml simple syrup

- ½ oz. | 15 ml fresh lemon juice
- 1 teaspoon | 5 ml fresh lime juice
- 2 dashes orange blossom soda

1. Chill a collins glass. Combine all of the ingredients, except for the soda, in a cocktail shaker.

2. Dry-shake without ice, then wet-shake with ice, very hard (but not too hard).

3. Pour the cocktail into the chilled collins glass, top with soda, wait 1 minute, then top up with more soda for a beautiful rise above the glass rim.

CANE OF THE CROP

THE D'S BAR AND DINING
359 ILLAWARRA RD, MARRICKVILLE

The rich tapestry of Asian culture is celebrated at The D's Bar and Dining in Marrickville, which fuses traditional flavors with Western culinary techniques. The philosophy of yin and yang is ingrained in Asian cuisine and is embraced at The D's in its pairing of cocktails with the delectable food offerings. The venue's grand double entry doors face lively Illawarra Road, and the corner location provides a great vantage point to watch the bustling neighborhood. Inspired by the vibrant energy of New York City, the bar has been meticulously crafted to emulate its allure, from the design elements to the carefully selected furnishings and the entertainment, which includes live jazz on Friday and Saturday nights.

GLASSWARE: Wineglass
GARNISH: Lychee, pineapple wedge

- 2 oz. | 60 ml sugarcane syrup
- 1½ oz. | 45 ml vodka
- 1 oz. | 30 ml orange juice
- ⅓ oz. | 10 ml lychee juice
- ⅓ oz. | 10 ml ginger syrup

1. Add all of the ingredients to a cocktail shaker and wet-shake with ice.

2. Single-strain the cocktail into a wineglass.

3. Garnish with lychee and a pineapple head.

THE F**KTINI

MARY'S
6 MARY ST, NEWTOWN

The Espresso Martini was created by bartender Dick Bradsell at the Soho Brasserie in London in the 1980s, when he was asked by a beautiful woman to make her a drink that would "f**k me up and then wake me up." Sydney loves a coffee and the staff at Mary's have turbo-charged it so it can be enjoyed it at 1 a.m. with friends. Also, as they note, it's delicious in cocktail form. Jake Smyth and Kenny Graham opened their first restaurant together in April 2013 with Mary's, a former medical clinic on a small backstreet of Newtown turning out up to 10,000 burgers per week. The pair describe themselves as builders of venues, ambassadors of the arts, curators of culture, mavens of musical madness, and disciples to the lost art of a night out. Mary's now has four venues, at Newtown, Circular Quay, Castle Hill, and the Entertainment Quarter in Sydney's East.

GLASSWARE: Coupette glass

- 1½ oz. | 45 ml vodka
- ⅔ oz. | 20 ml freshly brewed espresso
- ¼ oz. | 7.5 ml simple syrup

1. Combine all of the ingredients in a Boston shaker.

2. Half fill with ice.

3. Shake it until your arms hurt!

4. Single-strain the drink into a coupette.

COASTAL NEGRONI

LONGSHORE
5 KENSINGTON ST, CHIPPENDALE

T he menu at Longshore is inspired by coastal ingredients and techniques from around the world and showcases the best of Australian
produce. For example, the infusion of roasted kombu adds a touch of
umami, and the finger lime garnish celebrates the city's culinary identity.

❖

GLASSWARE: Lowball glass
GARNISH: Fresh finger lime

- 1 oz. | 30 ml Roasted
  Kombu–Infused Gin (see
  recipe)
- 1 oz. | 30 ml Poor Toms
  Imbroglio Amaro
- 1 oz. | 30 ml MAiDENii Dry
  Vermouth

1. Combine all of the ingredients in a mixing glass and stir with ice
until the dilution is right.

2. Strain the cocktail over a large ice cube in a lowball glass.

3. Garnish with fresh finger lime.

ROASTED KOMBU–INFUSED GIN: Roast ⅓ oz. (10 grams) kombu
at 340°F (170°C) for 45 minutes, then let it cool. Infuse the roasted
kombu into 1 oz. (30 ml) Marrickville's Poor Toms Sydney Dry Gin at
room temperature for 4 hours, strain, and put aside.

CARLA'S MARTINI

YOUNG HENRYS
76 WILFORD ST, NEWTOWN

Young Henrys is a proudly independent brewery, distillery, and tasting bar located in an open industrial space near the thriving nighttime precinct on Enmore Road. One of the bar's signature gin serves is Carla's Martini, which the staff describe as being a "very Sydney (or in particular, Newtown) cocktail" because it allows for infinite creativity and personal spins. Want to add something different to a classic? Try a grapefruit spritz and twist! Like olives? Go dirty! Prefer fruity drinks? Add grapefruit juice! Young Henrys' only rule for mixing Martinis is they must always be served ice cold. Being pre-batched means Carla's Martini isn't shaken or stirred with ice. Instead, just make it and store it in the freezer until the bottle goes frosty, then it's good to go! This recipe makes two cocktails.

GLASSWARE: Martini glass

GARNISH: As desired (see options)

- 3 oz. | 90 ml Young Henrys Noble Cut Gin, frozen
- 1 oz. | 30 ml ice water
- ½ oz. | 15 ml Regal Rogue Lively White Vermouth

1. Stir all of the ingredients together in a mixing glass.

2. Pour the mixture into a martini glass then customize as desired (see right).

DIRTY: Add your desired amount of olive brine to the recipe and garnish with olives.

TWISTY MISTY: Zest a pink grapefruit rind over the top of the cocktail and garnish with the rind.

GOODTIME GRAPEFRUIT: Add ½ oz. (15 ml) (per serve) of fresh pink grapefruit juice to the cocktail and garnish with a grapefruit rind.

THE DRUNKEN BOTANIST

MR WATKIN'S BAR
467 HIGH ST, PENRITH

Sydney loves gin and it is a love affair that has been brooding for the past decade. Pairing the unique and floral botanicals of Sydney gins against crème de violette, elderflower, and lime makes The Drunken Botanist a crowd favorite at Mr Watkin's. Bar manager Liam Hayward says clarified lime juice takes the cocktail to a whole new level: "Clarifying our citrus creates a beautiful cosmic purple hue and gives the drink a smooth and delicate mouthfeel as well as the perfect balance of flavors," he says.

GLASSWARE: Coupe glass

- 1 oz. | 30 ml gin
- ½ oz. | 15 ml crème de violette
- ½ oz. | 15 ml elderflower liqueur
- ½ oz. | 15 ml Clarified Lime Juice (see recipe)

1. Wet-shake all of the ingredients together in a cocktail shaker.

2. To serve, double-strain the cocktail into a coupe.

CLARIFIED LIME JUICE: Line a fine-mesh strainer with a coffee filter and place it over a bowl. Pour lime juice, as needed, into the coffee filter and allow it to filter through.

SOUR NEGRONI

PLEASURE CLUB
324 KING ST, NEWTOWN

Recently opened Pleasure Club is a live music bar with a 4 a.m. license, the first of its kind issued in 100 years in Newtown. The inspiration for the bar was born when the world opened up again following the pandemic and the team from hospitality group Odd Culture journeyed to the United States to satiate their appetite for new experiences. The result is a cool pastiche of Hollywood rock 'n' roll, LA weirdness, the soulful sounds of Preservation Hall in New Orleans, blues, burlesque, and beyond. Group beverage manager Jordan Blackman says this Sour Negroni is a very "Sydney" drink, and easily one of the most ordered cocktails across Odd Culture's venues. "I thought there would be no better way to make it Odd Culture than to make it sour, playing into our love for wild ales," he says. "Sans lemon juice, we cut the vermouth with kriek lambic, a traditional Belgian wild ale with sour cherries, which adds red fruit, acid, and oak, before further acidifying the liquid with citric, malic, and tartaric acids for further complexity." The recipe is for a large batch, designed to be shared with friends. Any quality sweet vermouth can be substituted for the Partida Creus.

GLASSWARE: Rocks glass

GARNISH: Lemon or grapefruit twist

- 2½ quarts | 2.5 liters Kriek Vermut (see recipe)
- 1½ quarts | 1.5 liters London dry gin
- 25⅓ oz. | 750 ml Campari
- 25⅓ oz. | 750 ml Aperol

1. In a large container, mix together all of the ingredients.

2. Serve the cocktail over ice in rocks glasses and garnish with twists of lemon or grapefruit.

KRIEK VERMUT: In a large container, mix together 2½ quarts (1.5 liters) Boon Brouwerij Kriek Mariage Parfait Beer, 25⅓ oz. (750 ml) Partida Creus MUZ Natural Vermut, 1¾ oz. (50 grams) granulated sugar, 1 oz. (30 grams) citric acid, and 7⁄10 oz. (20 grams) malic acid, tartaric acid until the acids and sugar dissolve.

CARDINALE SIN

NICK & NORA'S
LEVEL 26/45 MACQUARIE ST, PARRAMATTA

The idea behind Nick & Nora's was to make people feel like they've stepped into the house of Nick and Nora, a fictional crime-fighting duo from the 1934 film *The Thin Man*. The rooftop space offers opulence and *Mad Men* glamor combined with views of the Parramatta skyline and a lavish cocktail list. Claudia Cardinale was an Italian-born starlet and sex symbol in the 1960s. This crisp and bubbly tipple named in her memory performs double duty—on the cusp of being both a dessert and boozy refined refreshment.

GLASSWARE: Coupette glass

- 1 oz. | 30 ml Bombay Sapphire sweetened with lemongrass
- 2¼ oz. | 100 ml sparkling wine
- 1 scoop lemon myrtle sorbet

1. Pour gin into a coupette glass.
2. Pour bubbles of choice into a carafe to be served on the side.
3. Add scoop of sorbet to the drink.
4. Serve with a napkin and spoon.

GLOSSARY OF NATIVE AUSTRALIAN COCKTAIL INGREDIENTS

Eucalyptus	The eucalyptus is an Australian evergreen tree. Health food stores normally stock eucalyptus oil.
Finger lime	Finger limes contain caviar-like beads filled with tart juice. They can be substituted with regular limes or key limes.
Lemon myrtle	Lemon myrtle grows naturally in the subtropical rainforests of Australia. It has a fresh fragrance of creamy lemon and lime. Kaffir lime leaf and lemon verbena have similar flavor profiles to lemon myrtle.
Lemon squash	This traditional Australian drink is made from a sweetened lemon concentrate and water. Try substituting with a lemon-flavored soda or soft drink.
Lilly pilly	Lilly pilly berries have a sweet-tart flavor with spice-filled notes reminiscent of cloves and cranberries.
Pepperberry	Pepperberry is four or five times hotter than black pepper and has a strong mineral-like taste. Try a mix of black pepper and Sichuan pepper as a substitute.
Wattleseed	Wattleseeds are roasted and ground to give a distinctly coffee-like aroma and flavor. Try using ground coffee beans in the same quantity in a recipe.

Acknowledgments

Thank you to the bar managers, bartenders, and owners who generously contributed their fantastic recipes and photos to this book . . . and to Margot Date for helping me convert all those milliliters to ounces.

I will be forever grateful to my partner, David Fuller, for his patience and support as I wrestled with hundreds of cocktail recipes, images, and interviews over endless nights and weekends.

Thank you to the team at Cider Mill Press for their guidance and expertise, including Buzz Poole, Jeremy Hauck, and Lindy Pokorny.

And cheers to Sydney for serving up so many world-class bars in such stunning locations, staffed by some of the most talented bartenders in the business.

About the Author

Alana House is the founder and editor of Drinks Digest, a website focused on drinks news and the Australian bar scene. She has lived in Sydney for more than twenty-five years and has been a drinks writer for more than nine years.

Prior to her career in drinks, Alana worked in women's lifestyle magazines, including *Australian Cosmopolitan* and *Singapore Harper's Bazaar*. She also edited magazines ranging from *Singapore CLEO* to *Everyday Food* and *Woman's Day*. During her subsequent digital career, Alana has been an editor and content creator at leading Australian news and lifestyle websites including Mamamia and Escape.

Discover more about Australian cocktails and the talented bartenders behind them at www.drinksdigest.com.

Photo Credits

Pages 1, 3, 6, 13, 15, 16, 22, 23, 210–211, and 238–239 used under official license from Shutterstock.com.

Pages 8 and 10 courtesy of the State Library of New South Wales.

Page 11 courtesy of the National Library of Australia.

All other images courtesy of the respective bars and restaurants.

Index

—ABOUT CIDER MILL PRESS BOOK PUBLISHERS—

Good ideas ripen with time. From seed to harvest, Cider Mill Press brings fine reading, information, and entertainment together between the covers of its creatively crafted books. Our Cider Mill bears fruit twice a year, publishing a new crop of titles each spring and fall.

"Where Good Books Are Ready for Press"
501 Nelson Place
Nashville, Tennessee 37214
cidermillpress.com

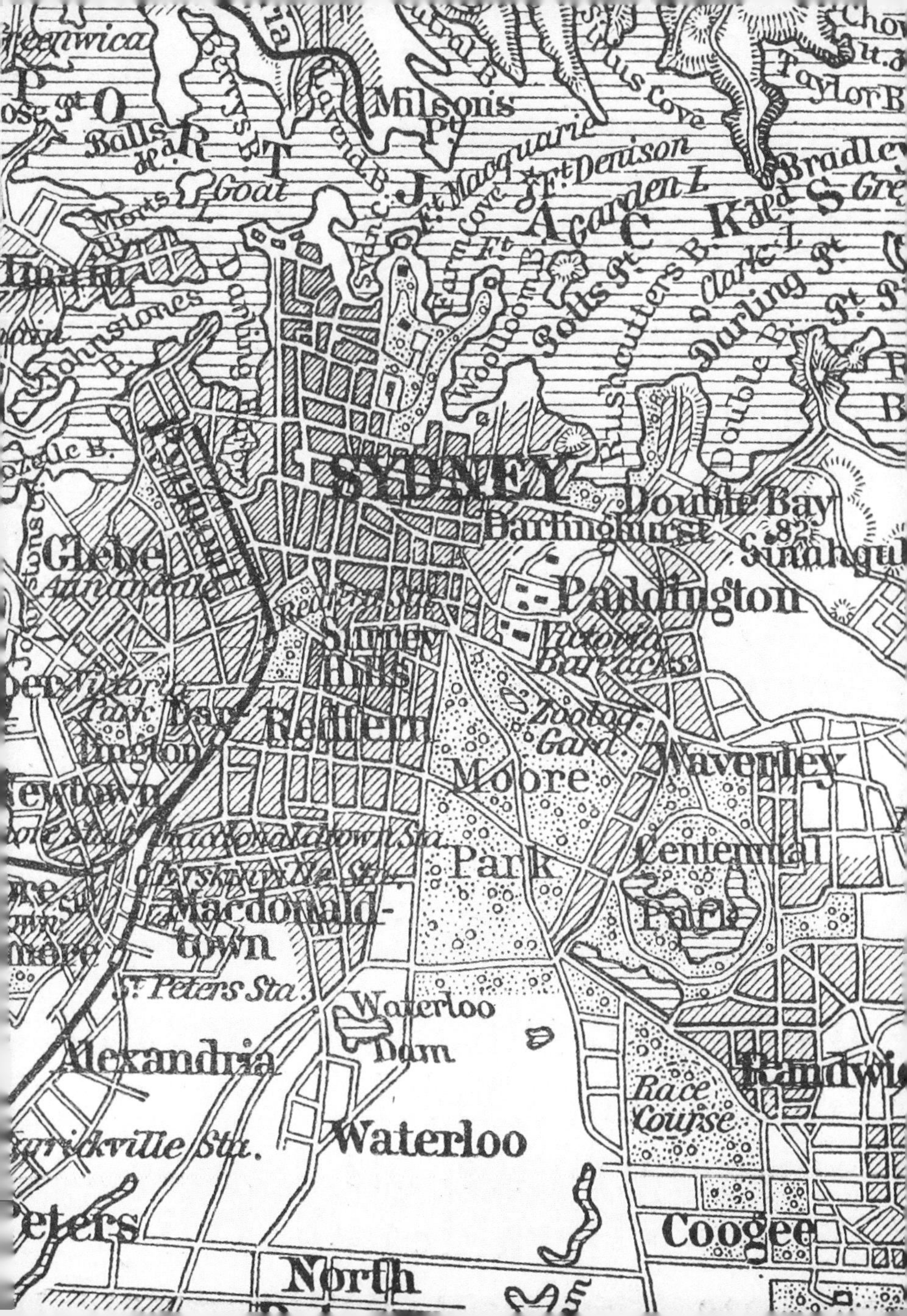
Milsons Pt.
Ft. Macquarie
Ft. Denison
Farm Cove
Garden I.
Goat I.
Balls H.d R.
Johnstones B.
Woolloomooloo B.
Rushcutters B.
Clark I.
Darling Pt.
Double B.
Bradleys
SYDNEY
Double Bay
Darlinghurst
Glebe
Annandale
Paddington
Surrey Hills
Victoria Barracks
Redfern
Zoolog. Gard.
Moore
Park
Waverley
Newtown
Centennial
Park
Macdonald-town
St. Peters Sta.
Waterloo
Dam
Alexandria
Race
Course
Waterloo
Peters
Coogee
North

Greenwich Pt
P O
Long Nose Pt
Balls Head
R T
Milsons Pt
Cockatoo
R.
Spectacle I.
Berrys B.
Ft. Macqu
Snapper
Morts Dk
Goat
Farm Cove
Ft.
Woolloomooloo B.
Balmain
W.Balmain
Johnstones B.
Iron Cove
SYDNE
Da
Leichhardt
Broughton
Rozelle B.
Blackwattle B.
Glebe
Annandale
Redfern Sta.
Surrey Hills
Canterbury Rd.
Park Paddington
Redfern
Moo
Par
Sydenham
Newtown
Newtown Sta.
Stanmore Sta.
Stanmore
Newtown
Macdonald-town
Macdonaldtown Sta.
Petersham Sta.
Norwood
Enmore
Dulwich Hill
St. Peters Sta.
Waterloo Dam
Marrickville
Rd. Sta.
Alexandria
Marrickville Sta.
Cooks R. Sta.
Waterloo
St. Peters